LIVING WITH
ADHD

By Nicole Horning

Portions of this book originally appeared in *ADHD* by Barbara Sheen.

Published in 2019 by
Lucent Press, an Imprint of Greenhaven Publishing, LLC
353 3rd Avenue
Suite 255
New York, NY 10010

Designer: Deanna Paternostro
Editor: Jennifer Lombardo

Cataloging-in-Publication Data

Names: Horning, Nicole.
Title: Living with ADHD / Nicole Horning.
Description: New York : Lucent Press, 2019. | Series: Diseases and disorders | Includes glossary and index.
Identifiers: ISBN 9781534563698 (pbk.) | ISBN 9781534564596 (library bound) | ISBN 9781534563681 (ebook)
Subjects: LCSH: Attention-deficit hyperactivity disorder–Juvenile literature.
Classification: LCC RJ506.H9 H67 2019 | DDC 618.92'8589–dc23

Printed in the United States of America

CPSIA compliance information: Batch #BS18KL: For further information contact Greenhaven Publishing LLC, New York, New York at 1-844-317-7404.

Please visit our website, www.greenhavenpublishing.com. For a free color catalog of all our high-quality books, call toll free 1-844-317-7404 or fax 1-844-317-7405.

CONTENTS

Illness is an unfortunate part of life, and it is one that is often misunderstood. Thanks to advances in science and technology, people have been aware for many years that diseases such as the flu, pneumonia, and chicken pox are caused by viruses and bacteria. These diseases all cause physical symptoms that people can see and understand, and many people have dealt with these diseases themselves. However, sometimes diseases that were previously unknown in most of the world turn into epidemics and spread across the globe. Without an awareness of the method by which these diseases are spread—through the air, through human waste or fluids, through sexual contact, or by some other method—people cannot take the proper precautions to prevent further contamination. Panic often accompanies epidemics as a result of this lack of knowledge.

Knowledge is power in the case of mental disorders, as well. Mental disorders are just as common as physical disorders, but due to a lack of awareness among the general public, they are often stigmatized. Scientists have studied them for years and have found that they are generally caused by hormonal imbalances in the brain, but they have not yet determined with certainty what causes those imbalances or how to fix them. Because even mild mental illness is stigmatized in Western society, many people prefer not to talk about it.

Chronic pain disorders are also not well understood—even by researchers—and do not yet have foolproof treatments. People who have a mental disorder or a disease or disorder that causes them to feel chronic pain can be the target of uninformed opinions. People who do not have these disorders sometimes struggle to understand how difficult it can be to deal with the symptoms. These disorders are often termed "invisible illnesses" because no one can see the symptoms; this leads many people to doubt that they exist or are serious problems. Additionally, people who have an undiagnosed disorder may understand that they are experiencing the world in a different way than their peers, but they have no one to turn to for answers.

Misinformation about all kinds of ailments is often spread through personal anecdotes, social media, and even news sources. This series aims to present accurate information about both physical and mental conditions so young adults will have a better understanding of them. Each volume discusses the symptoms of a particular disease or disorder, ways it is currently being treated, and the research that is being done to understand it further. Advice for people who may be suffering from a disorder is included, as well as information for their loved ones about how best to support them.

With fully cited quotes, a list of recommended books and websites for further research, and informational charts, this series provides young adults with a factual introduction to common illnesses. By learning more about these ailments, they will be better able to prevent the spread of contagious diseases, show compassion to people who are dealing with invisible illnesses, and take charge of their own health.

INTRODUCTION

A REAL DISORDER

Attention-deficit/hyperactivity disorder (ADHD) is a widely misunderstood disorder. According to the *Diagnostic and Statistical Manual of Mental Disorders, Fifth Edition (DSM-5)*, which is the manual health experts use to diagnose disorders such as ADHD, 5 percent of children have ADHD. However, according to the Centers for Disease Control and Prevention (CDC), that number is much higher; the CDC found that 11 percent of children between the ages of 4 and 17 (6.4 million) have been diagnosed with ADHD. In addition, the number of diagnoses has continued to increase throughout the years—from 7.8 percent in 2003 to 9.5 percent in 2007 to 11 percent in 2012. Despite these increasing figures, the amount of publications on ADHD, and the accommodations and modifications in place for millions of students in the United States, many continue to believe the disorder does not exist. There are even books that state the disorder does not exist, and this literature as well as statements repeating this false information can be extremely hurtful to people with the disorder and those around them that help them through each day.

People say ADHD does not exist for various reasons; for example, some claim that "the symptoms are caused by poor parenting, food additives, or 21st century life in the fast lane, lack of physical activity, or that they're just kids being kids, albeit less manageable than most."[1] However, what experts and parents say about these doubters is that they simply have not experienced ADHD firsthand.

Harmful Labels

Restlessness, impulsiveness, and inattentiveness can affect almost everyone at one time or another. What distinguishes individuals with ADHD from the rest of the population is that their symptoms are more frequent, persistent, and severe than those of other people, and these symptoms impair their lives in some way. However, because nearly everyone exhibits ADHD-like symptoms occasionally, many individuals with ADHD spend years not knowing they have a medical condition, and therefore, they can be greatly misunderstood by friends, family, teachers, employers, and coworkers. People may become frustrated with them, and they may be called lazy. Such labels can be hurtful to individuals with ADHD and may cause them to doubt themselves. Making matters worse, when people with ADHD try and fail to control their behavior without medical help, their belief in themselves may decrease even further. As television host Ty

Reality TV star Ty Pennington has been vocal about his ADHD diagnosis. This can help remove the stigma surrounding the disorder.

Pennington said of his ADHD before he was treated, "What happens is my confidence just kept waning and waning ... It wasn't until I finally got treated ... that I realized ... I actually do have a talent ... and I actually can make something of myself."[2]

Questioning ADHD's Existence

In addition to denying ADHD's existence, some people claim its symptoms are caused by things such as modern technology. They believe the increasing use of smartphones and computers has shortened children's attention spans and that this could be fixed by things such as putting away the phone, getting more physical activity, or simply trying harder to exercise self-control. However, ADHD has been around long before the 21st century. According to a *TIME* magazine article,

> We're ... asked from a very young age to be still, nearly motionless, except for the tapping of our fingers on the computer keys. Ours is not a society tolerant of perpetual motion or daydreaming ... But ADHD isn't a disorder of the modern age. It may have been first described in the medical literature in 1763 by Scottish physician Sir Arthur Crichton, who observed patients so unable to focus that "the barking of dogs, an ill-tuned organ, or the scolding of women, are sufficient to distract patients of this description to such a degree, as almost approaches the nature of delirium." Those patients, he noted, referred to their own symptoms, including anger "bordering on insanity," as "the fidgets."[3]

The argument that ADHD does not exist also falls apart when the United States is compared to other countries with different cultures. The disorder is "found in developing countries, where the information speed is slower and the requirement to be sedentary [inactive] 24/7 doesn't exist."[4]

Misconceptions that deny the seriousness of ADHD and the need to treat it keep some individuals from seeking professional help. They may cause some parents of children with ADHD to feel inadequate. As one person with ADHD wrote of their experience with the disorder, "Because ADHD is not a visible medical disorder people don't understand that it is just as disabling as those that are very visible. It requires understanding and acceptance that people with ADHD need some accommodations at times to perform to their potential."[5]

One of the misconceptions about ADHD is that it can be overcome by physical activity. Although exercising helps maintain a healthy body and has other positive benefits, exercise is not a way to "cure" someone with ADHD.

Societal Impact

The same lack of understanding about ADHD also impacts society. Left uncontrolled, ADHD can cause a multitude of problems. A 2014 Harvard newsletter reported that 52 percent of adults with the disorder say they use drugs recreationally. Researchers think individuals self-medicate with these substances to soothe their ADHD symptoms.

Unmanaged ADHD also has a financial impact. According to ADHD expert Russell A. Barkley, an estimated 35 percent of individuals with the disorder drop out of high school. Without a diploma, they may find it difficult to pursue career goals. Moreover, people with ADHD may have trouble holding jobs. Due to restlessness or impulsivity, they may switch jobs frequently or their employer may misunderstand the problems that are affecting their employee. However, the person with ADHD may simply be in the wrong career field or require accommodations, such as a distraction-free environment or an organized workflow, to perform their job to the best of their ability. According to the American Psychological Association's (APA) Center for Organizational Excellence, "Research suggests that people with ADHD are often underutilized, underemployed, and in jobs that are below their actual capabilities. Often, how they're functioning may not reflect how smart and capable they actually are."[6]

Education to Remove Misconceptions

Educating the public about what ADHD is and how people with ADHD are affected by the disorder is the best way to destroy harmful misconceptions. It is also the best way to support patients and their families. Knowledge about the condition can help people better understand ADHD and the behaviors associated with it and provide support. It can help people with the disorder overcome negative self-perceptions and seek the help they need. "Everyone who has [ADHD] can sculpt a fulfilling joyful life," wrote ADHD experts Edward M. Hallowell and John J. Ratey, both of whom have the disorder. "Doing so starts in your head ... You need knowledge ... Knowledge of what is truly going on can restore confidence and inspire hope."[7]

CHAPTER ONE

UNDERSTANDING ADHD

ADHD is not caused by vaccines, too much sugar, video games, television watching, or parenting style—although stressful home environments, possibly with parents who do not accept ADHD as a real diagnosis, can make the situation worse. Rather, ADHD is a complicated condition and the exact cause is unknown. However, research points strongly to ADHD having genetic causes—it is one of the psychiatric disorders most often passed down among families. According to the website Health.com,

> In fact, a child with ADHD is four times as likely to have had a relative who was also diagnosed with ADHD, and results from studies of multiple twins indicate that ADHD often runs in families. Ongoing research is looking to pinpoint the genes responsible for ADHD. A [2010] study by scientists at Cardiff University in Wales found that children with ADHD are more likely to have missing or duplicated segments of DNA.[8]

ADHD is a disorder that is marked by three things: impulsivity, hyperactivity, and inattention. It is important to note that while everyone may experience these things occasionally, ADHD significantly affects the lives of those who have it and can greatly impact the way a person functions in their day-to-day life. In addition, ADHD is not just experienced during childhood—it can also carry over into the teenage and adult years. Furthermore, it also affects women differently than men.

A misconception surrounding ADHD is that it is caused by too much time playing video games or watching television. However, numerous scientific studies show otherwise.

Signs of ADHD

While everyone may experience some inattention and fidgeting occasionally, these traits significantly affect the life of a person with ADHD. In addition, some of the signs of ADHD may point to other learning disabilities. Therefore, ADHD is not something that can be self-diagnosed or self-treated. It is something that requires the input of medical personnel and a personalized treatment plan, in addition to a personalized education plan to accommodate for how the disorder is affecting the student.

According to the National Institute of Mental Health (NIMH), people with ADHD may exhibit the following symptoms:

- *Overlook or miss details, make careless mistakes in schoolwork, at work, or during other activities*

- *Have problems sustaining attention in tasks or play, including conversations, lectures, or lengthy reading*

- *Seem to not listen when spoken to directly*

- *Fail to … follow through on instructions, fail to finish schoolwork, chores, or duties in the workplace, or start tasks but quickly lose focus and get easily sidetracked*

- *Have problems organizing tasks and activities, such as doing tasks in sequence, keeping materials and belongings in order, keeping work organized, managing time, and meeting deadlines*

- *Avoid or dislike tasks that require sustained mental effort, such as schoolwork or homework, or for teens and older adults, preparing reports, completing forms, or reviewing lengthy papers*

- *Lose things necessary for tasks or activities, such as school supplies, pencils, books, tools, wallets, keys, paperwork, eyeglasses, and cell phones*

- *Become easily distracted by unrelated thoughts or stimuli*

- *Forgetful in daily activities, such as chores, errands, returning calls, and keeping appointments[9]*

People with ADHD can easily become distracted while doing tasks such as studying or sitting in a classroom.

Additionally, the person with ADHD may exhibit signs such as frequent fidgeting while seated, getting up and moving around a room when the expectation is that they stay seated, feeling restless, running around in inappropriate situations, inability to play or work on hobbies quietly, being constantly on the go, and nonstop talking. They may have trouble waiting for their turn, or they may blurt out answers to questions before the question has been completed. In addition, they may finish others' sentences or speak without waiting for their turn in the conversation.

Structural Differences in the Brain

The most commonly held theory about the cause of ADHD is that the brains of individuals with ADHD have chemical, structural, or functional differences, or a combination of these differences, compared to those of people without the disorder. The cause of these differences has not been established. Because ADHD tends to run in families, scientists think that in most—but not all—cases, an inherited gene or genes is responsible. So far, one specific gene has not been identified, but a number of genes involved with brain chemistry, structure, and function have been. Errors in any of these genes may make individuals more likely to develop ADHD.

In 2010, scientists at Cardiff University in Wales, United Kingdom (UK), studied 366 children with ADHD and compared these results to 1,047 people without ADHD. The researchers looked for copy number variants (CNVs), which are missing or duplicated segments of deoxyribonucleic acid (DNA). For their study, they limited the analysis to rare CNVs that would only be present in small portions of the population. The study found that the duplicated and missing DNA segments were twice as common in people with ADHD as in those without it. In addition, the rare segments they studied were five times as common in people with ADHD and other intellectual disabilities. An interesting finding of the study was that some CNVs overlapped with DNA sections that have been suspected of playing a role in autism and schizophrenia. Even though these disabilities are all believed to be separate, the researchers in Cardiff believe there could be a shared biological base for the disorders.

While these findings are interesting to scientists and non-scientists alike, there are some researchers who are not fully convinced by the study. Dr. Josephine Elia is one of those people. She noted that the average intelligence quotient (IQ) of the children in the study who had ADHD was 86, while the control group of people without ADHD was made up of adult men and women with average IQs of 100. Since the adults' IQs were higher and rare CNVs are more common in people who have lower IQs, these rare CNVs would be even harder to find in the control group of people without ADHD. However, Elia did note the benefits of the study and stated that "studying CNVs remains an important research avenue. It may turn out to be not the number of CNVs, but rather which genes are missing or duplicated that plays a more important role in the development of ADHD."[10]

Other studies comparing the size and shape of the brains of people with ADHD to those without the

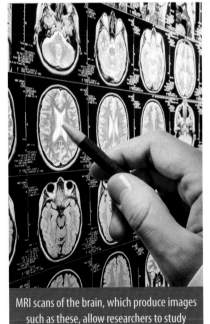

MRI scans of the brain, which produce images such as these, allow researchers to study differences between the brains of people with and without ADHD.

disorder indicate that structural differences in the brains of people with ADHD may be linked to the condition. A study conducted by NIMH from 1992 to 2002 compared the brains of 152 children with ADHD with 139 children of the same age and biological sex without the disorder. Each child's brain was scanned two to four times with magnetic resonance imaging (MRI) over the course of the study. The researchers found that, as a group, the brains of the children with ADHD were 3 to 4 percent smaller in all areas than those of the control group. The study also showed that the children with ADHD had a lower volume of white matter in their brains than the control group. White matter in the brain contains fibers that form the pathways neurotransmitters travel on. It is possible that this lack of white matter could limit the flow of information in the brain.

Other studies have looked at differences in particular parts of the brain. Some research has found that the basal ganglia—a part of the brain involved in motor control, emotions, and learning—is asymmetrical in some people with ADHD, whereas it is symmetrical in people without the disorder.

Another study, the results of which were released in 2017, found about five regions of the brain that may not be fully developed in children with ADHD. This confirms even more that ADHD is a disorder of the brain rather than caused by certain external environmental factors. The study was funded by the National Institutes of Health (NIH) along with the international ENIGMA ADHD Working Group. As of 2018, this study is the largest one on the brain differences between people with and without ADHD. MRI data from 1,529 people without ADHD and 1,713 people with ADHD was analyzed. The results found smaller brain volumes in areas of the brain called the putamen, caudate nucleus, hippocampus, nucleus accumbens, and amygdala. These differences were more significant for children.

The research both confirmed certain previous research and found new results. The structural differences in the putamen, which controls motor function, and caudate nucleus, which plays a role in how the brain stores and processes memories, were already known. However, the findings concerning the hippocampus, nucleus accumbens, and amygdala regions were new. The hippocampus controls emotions and memory storage, and the nucleus accumbens plays a role in classifying experiences as either positive or negative; when they are recalled later, the person can decide whether to seek out or avoid that particular experience. In particular, the changes in the amygdala, which also regulates emotions, were especially significant in this study, as they had not been found before. All of the study's findings prove that ADHD has a real, measurable effect on the brain.

Having ADHD, according to ADHD experts Edward M. Hallowell and John J. Ratey, is

> *like being supercharged all the time ... Your brain goes faster than the average brain. Your trouble is putting on the brakes. You get one idea, and you have to act on it, and then, what do you know, but you've got another idea before you finished up the first one, and so you go for that one, but of course a third idea intercepts the second and you just have to follow that one ... You have all these invisible [forces] pulling you this way and that, which makes it really hard to stay on task. Plus which, you're spilling over all the time. You're drumming your fingers, tapping your feet, humming a song, whistling, looking here, looking there, scratching, stretching, doodling.*[11]

Chemical Imbalance

The human brain is responsible for all of the body's physical, mental, and emotional functions. It is a complex organ made up of more than 100 billion cells called neurons and is divided into three large regions.

Each region of the brain is responsible for specific functions. For each region to do its job properly, neurons throughout the brain must communicate with each other. Chemicals known as neurotransmitters allow this to happen. Transported on proteins along wirelike pathways, neurotransmitters carry infor-

The Human Brain

The human brain is responsible for every function of the body, as well as a person's personality, emotions, thoughts, and views of the world. The brain weighs about 3 pounds (1.4 kg), making it one of the largest organs in the body.

Brain cells called neurons make up the brain's gray matter. The neurons transmit information in the form of electrical signals along a network of fibers called dendrites and axons, which make up the brain's white matter.

Information is sent to different parts of the brain. The cerebrum is the largest part of the brain. It has two halves, or hemispheres, which include four lobes. The frontal lobe controls speech, movement, learning, and emotions. The parietal lobe is involved in touch and sensing pain and temperature. The occipital lobe controls vision. The temporal lobe is involved with memory and hearing.

The cerebellum is the next largest part of the brain. It controls muscle movement and balance. It transmits information up and down the spinal cord.

The brain stem is the smallest part of the brain. It is located at the base of the brain. It controls life functions such as heartbeat, breathing, circulation, and sleep.

mation between the different regions of the brain. Without neurotransmitters, neurons could not communicate with each other, and the brain could not direct the body.

There are at least 50 types of neurotransmitters. Each carries different information, which controls diverse body functions or is involved with various emotional or mental functions. Two neurotransmitters called dopamine and norepinephrine carry information involved in attention, memory, impulsivity, self-control, organization, and activity level.

Research suggests that a chemical imbalance, which is simply too much or too little of one or more neurotransmitters, is at least part of the problem underlying most mental illnesses. For instance, abnormally high levels of dopamine are linked to schizophrenia and paranoia, while high levels of norepinephrine are linked to anxiety disorders. Scientists, therefore, theorize that a chemical imbalance plays a role in ADHD as well.

A 2007 study by the National Institute on Drug Abuse (NIDA) sought to prove this theory. Researchers performed brain scans on 19 adults with ADHD and 24 without the disorder. They found that the adults with ADHD released less dopamine into their brain pathways than those without the disease. Similar studies, which examined the brains of adults with ADHD using imaging tests, found similar results.

Determining Cause

Still other studies have found functional differences in the brains of people with ADHD. A 2005 study at the Institute of Psychiatry in London, England, challenged 16 adolescents with ADHD and 21 adolescents of the same age and biological sex without the disorder to perform a task that involved impulse control. A rapid form of MRI measured the level of activity in their brains while they were performing the task. The researchers found that the adolescents with ADHD had less brain activity in their frontal lobes—the part of the brain involved in impulse control and thought—than the control group. Other studies have shown similar results.

These studies have proven time and again that ADHD is not a result of environmental factors such as sugar or television. However, whether the cause is chemical, structural, functional, or a combination of these has not yet been established. More studies are necessary before scientists can reach a definitive conclusion.

Although scientists believe brain differences linked to ADHD are generally caused by an inherited gene, approximately one-fifth of all ADHD cases have been linked to other causes. Although these causes are acquired, they, too, affect the brain. For example, a fetus's developing brain can be adversely affected by exposure to unhealthy substances before birth. Babies born to mothers who smoked or drank alcohol during pregnancy are two and a half times more likely to develop ADHD than children born to mothers who did not engage in these activities.

Since brain cells continue developing throughout childhood, other causes can also lead to the development of ADHD. These include a severe head injury that causes a loss of consciousness, lack of oxygen to the brain as might occur in a near-drowning incident, lead poisoning before age three, a brain tumor, or an infection in the brain.

ADD versus ADHD

The terms "ADD" and "ADHD" are often used interchangeably, but the correct terminology according to the *DSM* is attention-deficit/hyperactivity disorder, or ADHD. The *DSM* used the term "attention deficit disorder" (ADD) until the fourth edition of the manual was released in 1994.

While ADHD was first recorded in the medical research of the late 1700s, it was not included in diagnostic manuals until the 1960s. As new medical research has been published, the diagnostic manuals have also been revised accordingly. The *DSM-5*, which was published in 2013, breaks ADHD into three subtypes: predominantly hyperactive-impulsive presentation; predominantly inattentive presentation; and combined presentation, which is the most common presentation of ADHD. Predominantly inattentive presentation is commonly called ADD, but the correct medical terminology for this would be inattentive ADHD or ADHD inattentive type. People with this type of ADHD generally still have trouble focusing, but they are less hyperactive and restless than people with the other two types.

ADHD Subtypes

Just as ADHD appears to have a number of causes, it also has a variety of symptoms. Although the condition is characterized by distractibility, inattentiveness, restlessness, and impulsivity, not every person with ADHD has all these symptoms. ADHD is the medical name given to three related conditions in which people have trouble regulating their behavior. Scientists think an individual's symptoms depend on specific differences in that person's brain. The APA classifies the three types of ADHD as predominantly inattentive presentation, predominantly hyperactive-impulsive presentation, and combined presentation. Each condition has different symptoms, and the combined presentation contains symptoms of both inattentive and hyperactive-impulsive types.

Predominantly Inattentive Presentation

Individuals with the inattentive type of ADHD have trouble consistently focusing their attention but generally have no problem with restlessness or impulse control. These individuals are easily distracted. Their minds tend to jump from subject to subject like rapidly changing channels on a television set. The symptoms of inattentive ADHD include:

- *Missing details and becoming distracted easily*

- *Trouble focusing on the task at hand*

- *Becoming bored quickly*

- *Difficulty learning or organizing new information*

- *Trouble completing homework or losing items needed to stay on task*

- *Becoming confused easily or daydreaming frequently*

- *Seeming not to listen when spoken to directly*

- *Difficulty following instructions*

- *Processing information more slowly and with more mistakes than peers*[12]

Such distractibility can make simple tasks such as listening to a lecture, completing an assignment, following or carrying on a conversation, or reading social cues difficult. In addition, to be diagnosed with inattentive type ADHD, the person has "to show at least six of the nine symptoms of inattention to be diagnosed … symptoms must be severe enough that they stop [the person] from completing everyday tasks and activities."[13]

However, problems with inattention do not occur all the time. People with the inattentive type of ADHD and those with the combination type of the disorder, which includes inattention among other symptoms, have the ability to hyperfocus. Hyperfocus generally occurs when an individual is performing an enjoyable activity. While hyperfocusing, individuals enter a state of extreme concentration in which they become thoroughly absorbed in an activity to the point of becoming completely unaware of time, place, or other activity around them. Hyperfocus is controversial, as not everyone with ADHD has it and there is limited scientific research on it. While hyperfocus can be used positively to complete tasks, the person may also intensely focus on an unproductive task. In addition, "unrestrained focus on unproductive tasks can lead to setbacks in school, lost productivity at work, or failed relationships … like all symptoms of ADHD, hyperfocus needs to be delicately managed.

Sometimes people with ADHD hyperfocus on a task they enjoy, such as writing, watching television, or playing a game.

When in a hyperfocused state, a child may lose track of time and the outside world may seem unimportant."[14] People who experience hyperfocus may need an enforced schedule, time markers or signals to refocus attention, or prioritization of tasks.

Predominantly Hyperactive-Impulsive Presentation

The hyperactive-impulsive type of ADHD is the least common form of the disorder—9 percent of all cases of ADHD fall into this group. The dominant symptoms are restlessness and impulsivity. This type of ADHD is more common in males than females, and researchers currently are unsure why. Individuals with hyperactive-impulsive ADHD are extremely restless, fidget a lot, talk excessively, and are generally very impatient. They have trouble taking turns and waiting in lines, may have frequent outbursts, and tend to interrupt when others are talking. Impulsiveness often leads individuals with this type of ADHD to develop risky, thrill-seeking behaviors that may take the form of gambling, compulsive shopping, or drug addiction. It leads them to act without considering the consequences.

At 17 years old, Blake E. S. Taylor published his memoir, *ADHD and Me: What I Learned from Lighting Fires at the Dinner Table*. As of 2017, he is the youngest person to write a published memoir about his experience with the disorder. He detailed one instance of his impulsivity in his memoir:

> *At home, I shattered the glass patio door twice with pebbles ... I didn't mean to shatter the glass. At the time, I was thinking of how entertaining it would be to see flying pebbles. A person with ADHD often does not think about cause and effect, does not connect the dots between thought, action, and consequence. You shoot pebbles because you want to see them fly, and*

you don't think about the objects in your path. The pebbles hit the windows, people get angry, and you get yelled at ... These all seem like independent— and unrelated—events in your mind.[15]

After completing his high school education, Taylor went to college at Columbia University's Vagelos College of Physicians and Surgeons. His goal is to remove the stigma, or negative view, of ADHD and change the public's view of the disorder by meeting with members of Congress, doing advocacy work, and speaking at public events.

A Lifelong Disorder

The symptoms of all three types of ADHD generally first appear in children younger than seven. Because ADHD symptoms affect people differently at different ages, for many years, experts believed ADHD was a disorder that children outgrew. This is not generally the case—60 percent of people with ADHD do not outgrow it. For them, it is a chronic disorder, which means it is a lifelong ailment that cannot be cured, only managed according to a plan decided upon with a medical professional. As these people age, however, the disorder impacts them differently. For instance, adults with ADHD appear to be less hyperactive. Instead of being outwardly restless, they often feel restless on the inside. Their hyperactivity frequently causes them to work a lot. They tend to overschedule their time and are constantly busy.

Impulsivity in adults often appears as a volatile, or explosive, temper, and inattentiveness is expressed in procrastination, poor time management, and disorganization. According to ADHD expert Russell A. Barkley,

We're not seeing anything that suggests a qualitative change in the disorder. What's changing for adults is the broadening scope of the impact. Adults have

more things they've got to do. We're especially see-
ing problems with time, with self-control, and with
planning for the future and being able to persist to-
wards goals. In adults, these are major problems.[16]

Interestingly, ADHD symptoms do disappear after puberty in 20 percent of people with ADHD. Scientists theorize that structural differences in the brains of these individuals caused them to develop ADHD. For unknown reasons, these individuals' brains are slower to develop than those of other people, but they do catch up eventually. When they do, their symptoms vanish.

Other Brain Disorders

Besides causing problems with attentiveness, hyperactivity and impulsivity, or a combination of both, ADHD is often accompanied by other brain-related disorders. For instance, 20 to 40 percent of people with ADHD have other learning disabilities. A learning disability is a neurological disorder in which people have problems with processing information. It is defined in the Individuals with Disabilities Education Act (IDEA) as

a disorder in one or more of the basic psychological
processes involved in understanding or in using lan-
guage, spoken or written, that may manifest itself
in an imperfect ability to listen, think, speak, read,
write, spell, or to do mathematical calculations ...
In other words, students with learning disabilities
(LD) have difficulty acquiring basic skills or aca-
demic content. Learning disabilities are character-
ized by intra-individual differences, usually in the
form of a discrepancy between a student's ability
and his or her achievement in areas such as read-
ing, writing, mathematics, or speaking. Although
they cannot be the primary problem, some students
with LD also have difficulties with social relations.

Intra-individual differences are differences within a student across academic areas.[17]

It is important to note that the definition of a learning disability varies among the general public and professionals, and even between different professional groups. For example, the above definition is for the general public and based on U.S. federal regulations.

In addition, many people with ADHD develop psychiatric disorders. This is called comorbidity, which is the presence of two or more conditions in the same patient. For example, according to the ADHD Institute, in one two-year study of 1,478 European children with ADHD, 32 percent developed depression, 44 percent developed anxiety, and 67 percent developed oppositional defiant disorder, which is a frequent, persistent pattern of irritability, anger, defiance, and arguing. Another study, which analyzed 14,825 children and teens, found that 52 percent of the participants had at least one comorbid disorder and 26.2 percent had two or more. Researchers think this may be because chemical imbalances provide a connection between ADHD and these illnesses. Indeed, some medicines used to treat depression are also effective in treating ADHD, which points to a biochemical link. On the other hand, it may be that some people develop other disorders, such as depression, as a response to the impact ADHD has on their lives.

Sleep disorders, too, often accompany ADHD. A link between sleep disorders and ADHD is not surprising, since ADHD symptoms make it hard for individuals to relax. These people say their thoughts race from one problem to another as soon as they turn out the lights. As a result, many people with ADHD are unable to fall asleep until the early hours of the morning. Once asleep, they tend to toss and turn. Many move around so much that they tear off their bed sheets. This may be why 80 percent of adults with ADHD say they have trouble waking up in the morning and are plagued with daytime sleepiness.

Sleep disorders may accompany ADHD and cause people with the disorder to fall asleep at inappropriate times and places, such as in class or the library, due to exhaustion.

Risk and Management

Anyone can have ADHD. Certain individuals, however, are at greater risk. A family history of the disorder greatly increases an individual's vulnerability to developing it. The reality is that there are still many unanswered questions about ADHD. It is a complicated condition that can cause diverse and often lifelong problems for those who have it. However, even though someone is diagnosed with ADHD, it does not mean they cannot have a fulfilling and productive life. The first step toward this is seeking help from a medical professional. With a doctor's help, the person with ADHD can create a plan to manage their ADHD, whether it involves medication, lifestyle changes, or a combination of both. In addition, there are services to help those with ADHD, such as laws that protect the person's rights and accommodations that can be worked into an education plan. However, before the person with ADHD can start receiving these accommodations, they need to be diagnosed.

CHAPTER TWO

DIAGNOSING ADHD

Diagnosing ADHD can be difficult. It requires multiple tests, and they are not quick and easy, such as blood or urine tests. Before a person can even take the tests, they must exhibit symptoms of ADHD for more than six months. ADHD diagnosis may include interviews, symptom and behavior rating, and observations. To diagnose ADHD, health care providers use the *DSM-5*, which provides a standard of how to diagnose ADHD and other disorders. The *DSM-5* ensures that people are correctly diagnosed and treated, and using it helps professionals determine the impact on public health the disorder has within a community.

Once the person is diagnosed, the health care professional will work with them to determine the appropriate medication. However, while ADHD is controversial because some people do not believe it actually exists, there is an additional level of controversy over whether ADHD medications are overprescribed. While the media promotes news stories about this medication controversy, there are also people who experience this very real disorder who may benefit from the medication. This debate within the medical community may make people with ADHD feel as though they do not have a voice.

Misdiagnosis

ADHD is difficult to diagnose with precision.

Because most people exhibit ADHD-like symptoms occasionally and ADHD symptoms can range from mild to extreme, some normal behaviors may get confused with that of ADHD. Some children may be inattentive, restless, and impulsive, but the difference with ADHD is that it greatly impacts the daily functioning of the individual and it occurs over a period of at least six months. Given that children can exhibit these traits occasionally even when they do not have a disorder, this six-month timespan of symptoms is very important. Not surprisingly, many people are misdiagnosed with the condition while others go through life with ADHD without ever being correctly diagnosed. According to the Anxiety and Depression Association of America (ADAA), "less than 20 percent of adults with ADHD have been diagnosed or treated, and only about one-quarter of those adults seek help."[18]

Adding to the problem, other psychiatric disorders share similar symptoms with ADHD. ADHD is often confused with these conditions. Issues such as hearing impairments, sleep disorders, sensory processing disorders (a condition that is marked by under- or oversensitivity to things such as movement, sound, taste, touch, sight, and smell), autism, low blood sugar levels, and bipolar disorder (a condition that is marked by extreme shifts in moods, from a high to a depressive low point) all share ADHD-like symptoms. In fact, 70 percent of individuals diagnosed with bipolar disorder also qualify for an ADHD diagnosis.

Traits of giftedness can also be confused with ADHD. Gifted individuals often appear inattentive or restless, but their inattention and restlessness are due to not being challenged enough. Gifted individuals "may talk a lot, have high levels of energy, and be impulsive or inattentive or distractible in some settings—similar to symptoms of ADHD. It's not unusual for gifted kids to struggle socially, have meltdowns over minor issues, or have unusual all-consuming interests."[19] While gift-ed children are believed to excel in their subjects at school, that is not always the case. A gifted child may be a troublemaker, a class clown, or a quiet person in the back row of the classroom. Frequently, the needs of these children are left unsupported, and they are not in classes that fit their needs and allow them to excel. Therefore, they may be misdiagnosed with medical conditions they do not have or not diagnosed at all for conditions they do have.

While gifted children and children with other con-ditions may be misdiagnosed with ADHD or children with ADHD may be diagnosed with other disorders, it is also extremely common for girls and women to not be diagnosed with ADHD at all. Statistics point to ADHD being more common in males, but part of the reasoning behind this is that girls may exhib-it signs of ADHD that are different and therefore not recognized as being part of the typical ADHD pattern of behavior.

Women and ADHD

Females are frequently not diagnosed with ADHD until they become adults. In addition, according to an article in *The Atlantic*, there are still around 4 mil-lion women who are not diagnosed with ADHD. Dr. Ellen Littman, author of *Understanding Girls with ADHD*, attributes the underdiagnosis of ADHD in girls and women to the early clinical studies of ADHD in the 1970s. At this time, the research was based on hyperactive boys who were taken to clinics—girls were severely underrepresented in these studies. Even later research on ADHD has been based on samples that consisted primarily of boys. According to Dr. Littman, "The diagnostic criteria were devel-oped based on those studies. As a result, those criteria over-represent the symptoms you see in young boys, making it difficult for girls to be diagnosed unless they behave like hyperactive boys."[20]

Dr. Meadow Schroeder, a professor of education with a background in psychology, also commented on this issue. In an article for CNN, she noted that the early signs of ADHD look different between girls and boys. While boys may be fidgeting in their seat, a hyperactive girl may take on the role of classroom helper and wander around between different desks. Even though having difficulty staying seated is a symptom of ADHD, it is often not applied to girls with ADHD because they are generally viewed as being helpful, not hyperactive or disruptive. In addition, adults may unintentionally have different expectations for boys and girls. Girls may be expected to be organized, achieve high grades, and generally avoid causing trouble. This gender stereotype can be harmful to girls because if they do not display these behaviors, they may be labeled with hurtful terms such as "ditzy" or "dramatic." Additionally, if ADHD explains their behavior, these gender stereotypes can prevent them from getting an accurate diagnosis. According to *The Atlantic*,

> *Women with the disorder tend to be less hyperactive and impulsive, more disorganized, scattered, forgetful, and introverted. "They've alternately been anxious or depressed for years," Littman says. "It's this sense of not being able to hold everything together"* ... *A [2012] study published in the* Journal of Consulting and Clinical Psychology *found that girls with ADHD have high rates of self-injury and suicide during their teenage years, bringing attention to the distinct severity of ADHD in females. In* Pediatrics, *a large population study found that the majority of adults with ADHD had at least one other psychiatric disorder, from alcohol abuse to hypomanic episodes to major depression. This poses a particular threat to females, for whom ADHD diagnoses tend to come later in life.*[21]

In addition, when girls or women are diagnosed with ADHD, the diagnosis may be met with skepticism and hurtful things can be said, such as pointing out that the person cannot possibly have ADHD because she is smart. This implies that people with ADHD are not smart and, similarly, that if the diagnosis were true, the girl in question would no longer be considered smart. In reality, people with ADHD are frequently just as intelligent as people without the disorder. If they get lower grades, it is generally because of their inability to concentrate on schoolwork or studying, not because they do not know how to do the work.

In her article for CNN, Dr. Schroeder provided a list of the different ways ADHD may manifest in girls. While these are not clinically accepted by the APA, they are additional symptoms to look for that may lead to a girl getting the diagnosis she needs. Dr. Schroeder's list includes:

- *Homework takes longer than it should. She forgets about it or is distracted by surfing the internet or texting her friends and ends up staying up late the night before an assignment is due to finish it.*

- *She is an inefficient student. While she appears to study for tests, her performance does not seem to match the time spent studying.*

- *She has weak reading comprehension. She can get facts from a text but does not make links between the ideas she reads. She misses details in instructions on assignments and tests.*

- *She struggles with friendships because she does not read social cues or follow conversations. Peers start to reject and isolate her or make fun of her.*

- *She forgets things she needs (e.g. dance shoes or soccer cleats). This is a classic sign but agreeable girls with ADHD will often have friends or adults who compensate for them (for example sharing a pen because she doesn't have one).*

- *She misplaces her things regularly (for example her phone, keys or bank card).*

- *She talks, and talks and talks.*

- *She does not run and climb about like boys but is the classroom helper and is social and chatty in class.*

- *She has lots of friends because she is fun to be around but when she tries to organize activities she seems anxious and indecisive. Her friends help her make decisions, find her things and keep her organized.*

- *She has great ideas and wants to start acting on them right away but does not finish projects or follow through.*

- *She is chronically late or is not ready when she needs to be.*

- *She channels hyperactivity by being involved in many extracurricular activities like swimming, school clubs and soccer.*

- *She does not seem to learn from consequences.*

- *She has wide swings in mood. One moment she is on top of the world and the next moment she is crushed because of a casual comment that is taken as harsh criticism.*[22]

While lists in articles online and questionnaires found on the internet can be helpful, it is best to seek a medical professional's help to get a proper diagnosis of a medical condition.

Creative Benefits

People with ADHD score higher on tests of creativity than the general population. This may be because the impulsiveness that many people with ADHD display compels them to take creative risks and decreases their inhibitions. This makes them unafraid to try something new or something that others might consider ridiculous. Impulsivity also allows them to ask questions that others might be too inhibited to ask, which might be the key to new ideas and solutions to problems.

In addition, inattention, which often leads to daydreaming, may be the first step in creative undertakings such as writing or painting. Wandering attention also allows individuals to view a problem from different angles, possibly seeing answers that more focused people who follow a more logical train of thought might miss. Indeed, people with ADHD often connect facts in unique ways.

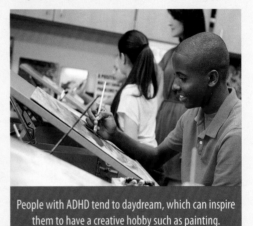

People with ADHD tend to daydream, which can inspire them to have a creative hobby such as painting.

Diagnostic Tests

What makes diagnosing ADHD all the more challenging is that, unlike medical conditions such as diabetes or cancer, there is no definitive diagnostic test for ADHD. Some physicians administer a brain scan, which can detect differences in brain structure and activity. However, brain differences that are linked to ADHD are also common in head injuries, schizophrenia, and other mental disorders. The tests, therefore, do not provide conclusive answers. For this reason, the American Academy of Child and Adolescent Psychiatry does not recommend imaging tests to diagnose ADHD.

In place of medical tests, physicians rely on several different assessment tools. The first is a behavioral history. This involves discussing the patient's

There is no single test to diagnose ADHD, the way blood tests can detect diabetes, for example. Instead, ADHD testing is a long process of interviews, rating scales, and medical exams to rule out other issues.

behavioral symptoms with the patient and close family members. It also involves gathering written or verbal descriptions of the patient's behavior from current and former teachers, in the case of children. Doctors also use a questionnaire known as the Conners Rating Scale. Adult patients and their spouses fill it out, and parents and teachers complete it for child patients. The questionnaire helps establish the type and severity of the patient's symptoms. Doctors also take the patient's medical history and administer a medical exam to rule out physical problems, such as vision or hearing disorders.

Once the possibility of other illnesses is eliminated, the doctor evaluates the patient's symptoms according to guidelines set in the *DSM-5*. By providing a checklist of symptomatic behaviors and the intensity and frequency of those behaviors, the book provides criteria for diagnosing different mental disorders, including ADHD.

First Line of Treatment

Once a diagnosis is made, medication is generally the first line of treatment. It does not cure ADHD or eliminate all the symptoms entirely, but it does lessen symptoms in 80 percent of those who take it.

Currently, there are two types of ADHD medications. Stimulants are the most common type. These drugs energize the body. Although it would seem that this is the last thing people with ADHD need, these drugs have an opposite effect on people with ADHD. They calm them down, decrease impulsiveness, and sharpen their focus. Scientists do not know exactly why this is so, but they do know that stimulants cause more dopamine to be released into pathways in the brain. This, scientists say, normalizes chemical

Medical Marijuana

As of early 2018, 29 states and Washington, D.C., have legalized marijuana for medical purposes. While medical marijuana is commonly used for illnesses such as cancer, HIV, and AIDS, it may also be helpful for those with ADHD. A 2013 study that was published in the *Journal of Substance Use and Misuse* examined "280 cannabis users and the main finding was that a higher proportion of users reported experiencing symptoms of ADD/ADHD when they were not self-medicating."[1] The people examined in the study had found that traditional medication was not effective for them and marijuana helped them deal with the hyperactivity and impulsivity of ADHD. The results of the study allowed researchers to push for additional resources to further study the link.

In a German study that monitored patients between 2012 and 2014, researchers examined the relationship between marijuana use and ADHD in 30 patients. The patients the researchers chose for this study were resistant to the traditional treatments for ADHD. The study reported,

In all 30 cases, patients reported improvements in a variety of ADD/ADHD symptoms including concentration and impulsivity. In other cases, patients saw an improvement in sleep. All patients used some form of cannabis flower and in 8 patients, they used dronabinol, a THC drug used to treat nausea and vomiting.[2]

Medical marijuana has been legalized in 29 states as of 2018. Researchers have looked into the benefits it may have for people with ADHD.

Even though the study sample was small, the researchers in the study felt that marijuana could be an effective treatment for some of the symptoms of ADHD, particularly if traditional medications are not proving effective for a patient. However, given that the study was so small, more research is needed to determine whether marijuana can be an effective component of ADHD treatment.

1. Brea Mosley, "How Medical Marijuana Can Help Those with ADD and ADHD Focus," *Salon*, June 3, 2017. www.salon.com/2017/06/03/how-medical-marijuana-can-help-those-with-add-and-adhd-focus_partner/.

2. Mosley, "How Medical Marijuana Can Help Those with ADD and ADHD Focus."

imbalances, helping the flow of information to the different parts of the brain.

Ritalin, Concerta, and Adderall are among the most common stimulants, but there are a number of others. These drugs are generally taken orally and take effect in about 20 minutes.

Depending on the particular medication and the dosage, the effects last from 3 to 12 hours. After this time, any positive effects wear off. Many people with ADHD prefer longer-acting medication since remembering to take medicine can be a problem for people with ADHD.

ADHD medication delivered through the skin directly into the bloodstream is long acting. This medication is administered via a patch that is worn on the patient's body for up to nine hours. Once it is removed, its effects continue for an additional three hours. At present, the patch is only available for use by children ages six to twelve.

The other type of medication that can treat ADHD is a drug called Strattera. It works by elevating the level of norepinephrine in the brain. It does this by keeping the proteins that carry norepinephrine from absorbing any of the neurotransmitter. Strattera, which is taken orally (by mouth), lasts all day.

Finding the Right Dosage

Prescribing medication for ADHD is not simple. It takes time to determine which medication and dosage best suit a particular patient. If the dosage is too high, patients tend to feel sleepy and slowed down; if it is too low, their symptoms do not decrease. What makes prescribing the right dosage all the more difficult is that the dosage depends on how fast the patient's body breaks down, or metabolizes, the drug. As a result, it is possible that a young child might require more frequent and larger amounts of an ADHD drug than a grown person. Generally, patients are started on the lowest dose of a medication. The dosage is then systematically altered until an effective level is reached.

Moreover, each person responds differently to different drugs. Often, patients must switch between medications until they find one that relieves their symptoms without causing other problems. According to Hallowell and Ratey,

> *Finding the right dose of the right medicine can take time. It is a process of trial and error, as we do not yet have any tests that can tell us in advance which medication will work best in a given individual or what dose will be the right one ... The goal is to get improvement in the negative symptoms like loss of focus or disorganization, without side effects.*[23]

According to many people with ADHD, the difference the correct medication makes in their ability to control their behavior is impressive. As Maria Yagoda wrote in *The Atlantic*,

> *I can't say that I know what part is ADHD, what part is me, or whether there's a difference. I can say that ADHD medication ... has granted me a base level of functionality; it has granted me the cognitive energy to sit at my jobs, to keep track of my schedule and most of my possessions, and to maintain a semblance of control over the ... fairly standard tasks that had overwhelmed me—like doing laundry, or finding a sensible place to put my passport.*
>
> *Medication is certainly not a cure-all, but when paired with the awareness granted by a diagnosis, it has rendered my symptoms more bearable—less unknown, less shameful.*[24]

However, while medication can largely change the ADHD symptoms in most people with the disorder, treatment should go beyond medication and also include other therapies. In addition, medication may not work for some people and, like other medications, ADHD medication comes with side effects.

Side Effects

Despite the help ADHD medicines provide, like all medications, they can cause side effects and present health risks. In the case of stimulants, among the most common side effects is loss of appetite. This can lead to an unhealthy weight loss. Lack of proper nutrition can weaken the immune system and slow growth patterns in children and adolescents. Growth patterns normalize, however, if treatment is stopped. Even taking breaks from medication, as some young people do during school vacations, appears to help.

Stimulants can also cause emotional sensitivity, irritability, headaches, and high blood pressure. Since high blood pressure can lead to heart attack and stroke, patients who have high blood pressure must be closely monitored if they wish to continue using the medication. In addition, some individuals experience what is known as a rebound effect shortly after the drug's effect wears off. This involves 30 to 60 minutes of increased hyperactivity, impulsivity, and constant talking.

Facial and vocal tics are another problem. Facial tics are sudden, repetitive, involuntary movements, such as winking, blinking, sniffling, lip licking, mouth opening and closing, and head movements. Vocal tics include throat clearing and coughing. Stimulants prescribed for ADHD cause facial and vocal tics in 9 percent of children. Tics can also develop in adults.

Some patients cease taking stimulant medication due to tics. Generally, once patients stop taking the medication, the tics disappear within a few months. However, in 1 percent of all cases, tics become chronic.

Some patients counteract tics by taking a medication called clonidine in combination with ADHD medication. Clonidine has its own side effects. For instance, if a dose is missed, it can result in dangerous fluctuations in a person's blood pressure.

Strattera poses still other issues. It can cause stomachaches, fatigue, dizziness, nausea, liver damage, mood swings, and suicidal thoughts. In a clinical trial, Eli Lilly, the manufacturer of Strattera, evaluated 2,200 children and adolescents. Strattera was given to 1,357 subjects, and a placebo, or sugar pill, was given to 843 subjects. There were 5 cases of suicidal thinking and 1 case of attempted suicide among the 1,357 taking Strattera, compared to 0 in the placebo group. Although this is a small percentage, the medication does present a risk. As a result, in September 2005, Eli Lilly added a warning to the product's label stating that the medication may cause suicidal thoughts in children and adolescents. For unknown reasons, there does not appear to be a similar risk to adults. Young people taking the drug must be closely monitored. They are advised to tell their health care provider, parent, or a close relative or friend if they develop suicidal thoughts and to stop taking the medication immediately.

The Controversy over Medication

Still another concern is that Ritalin can be used as a recreational drug because high doses of it produce a euphoric effect. Those who abuse it may include people with ADHD as well as those without the disorder who obtain it from people who have a prescription. Large doses of Ritalin can cause serious and even fatal side effects. These include hallucinations, seizures, strokes, dangerously high blood pressure, heart problems, and blood clots in the heart and lungs.

In addition to concern over drug abuse, there is also

significant controversy over the use of psychotropic medications in young people and whether they are being overprescribed. Some people have expressed concern about the fact that toddlers are taking psychotropic medication, among other medications. People who think these medications are overprescribed provide a variety of reasons, including:

> *Children with behavioral or emotional problems are being overmedicated by psychiatrists too busy to provide therapy, at the request of parents too busy to provide a healthy home environment. [The next theory] is to blame schools too busy to provide recess or activities for fidgety [children]. And usually the blame extends to the pharmaceutical companies that market medications in pursuit of profits.*[25]

In 2016, the CDC urged parents of preschool children who were diagnosed with ADHD to try behavioral therapies before medication. Less than half of the children the CDC advised to try behavioral therapies were receiving these services, but 75 percent of them were on medication. One of the reasons for this is how long each treatment takes to make a difference. Once the correct dosage of medication is found, the effects are quickly noticeable. However, behavioral therapies can take months of hard work—on the part of both parents and children—to start making a difference, although the CDC noted that the effects of behavioral therapies can last longer. However, the largest reason medication may be chosen over behavioral therapies is that these therapies are simply not available within a reasonable driving distance for families. Therefore, the only choice they have is to try medication first. In addition, many insurance companies do not cover alternative therapies such as behavioral therapies, leaving the family to pay out of pocket.

These recommendations by the CDC follow what other countries recommend for ADHD treatment, including behavioral therapy, counseling, and lifestyle changes, with medication as a last resort. However, the U.S. guidelines recommend medication as a first resort. In 2011, the American Academy of Pediatrics released a set of guidelines that started moving toward nonmedical interventions. The basis behind the CDC's concerns is the long-term effects of ADHD medications: "The long-term effects of those drugs on a young brain and body have not been well studied, and the side effects can be numerous, including poor appetite, sleeplessness, irritability and slowed growth."[26] Therefore, until more is known about ADHD medications and their long-term effects, the CDC recommends behavioral therapies and ADHD training for children under six who have been diagnosed with the disorder.

On the other side of the debate, NIMH pointed out,

> *Is it possible that the increased use of medication is not the problem but a symptom? What if more children were struggling with severe psychiatric problems and actually the problem was not overtreatment but increased need? Surely, if we discovered more children were being treated for diabetes or immune problems, we wouldn't blame the providers or the parents. We'd be asking what drives the increase in incidence.*[27]

A large part of the controversy over ADHD diagnosis and medication may come from the fact that emotional and behavioral disorders are not diagnosed in the same way as conditions such as diabetes or allergies. There is no definitive test that proves ADHD is present the way there is for diseases that can be diagnosed with a blood test or brain scan. Without what some may see as hard evidence of ADHD being present, they may misunderstand the situation and think children are being overdiagnosed and overmedicated.

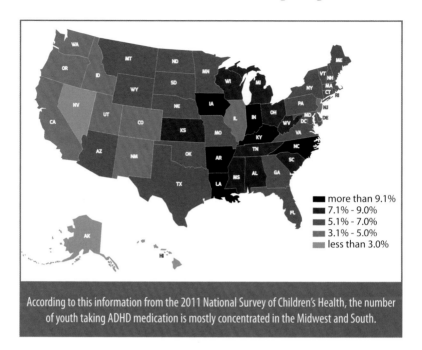

■	more than 9.1%
■	7.1% - 9.0%
■	5.1% - 7.0%
■	3.1% - 5.0%
■	less than 3.0%

According to this information from the 2011 National Survey of Children's Health, the number of youth taking ADHD medication is mostly concentrated in the Midwest and South.

However, the fact remains that medication can greatly help most people with ADHD, and people with other conditions, such as diabetes or allergies, are not denied the appropriate medications that help them live each day to their fullest. For some people with ADHD, however, medication does not eliminate all symptoms, or they may choose to more aggressively treat the condition. For these people, there are alternative therapies.

CHAPTER THREE

ALTERNATIVE TREATMENTS

While medication can help lessen ADHD symptoms, the person or their family may choose to also integrate alternative therapies. These alternate treatments should not be used alone, however. Research shows that merely participating in counseling or behavioral therapy does not fully treat ADHD symptoms. Instead, research shows that the best approach to treating ADHD is to use medication combined with other treatments.

Counseling Sessions

Talking to a mental health professional is a traditional form of treatment for people with ADHD. It is most effective when it is combined with medication. Combining counseling and other forms of mental health care, such as behavioral therapy, with medication to treat ADHD is known as a multimodal approach. It involves a team of people, including the patient, the patient's family, a physician, and a mental health professional.

Counseling helps individuals become more self-aware. During counseling sessions, patients talk about their innermost thoughts and feelings in a safe, non-judgmental atmosphere. Many people with ADHD have feelings of anger and frustration as a result of the disorder and the stigma society attaches to it. Talking to a counselor allows individuals to discuss these feelings and learn how to handle them. It also helps them discover their personal strengths and talents and come up with strategies that use their strengths to cope with the challenges that ADHD presents. Family, work, school, social, and behavioral issues can all be dealt with in this manner.

Counseling comes in many forms and settings. Psychologists, psychiatrists, and mental health counselors can all serve as a counselor or therapist. Therapy sessions can include individual counseling, family or couples counseling, group therapy, or a combination, depending on what works best for the patient.

Cognitive Behavioral Therapy

Other types of traditional therapy deal less with emotions and more with behavior. Cognitive behavioral therapy (CBT) is one of the most common forms of this type of treatment. It is a systematic approach to changing behavior that is especially effective with young children. In this therapy, children learn a set of rules about their behavior and actions. They are taught by using workbooks, talking with mental health professionals, and role-playing. At the same time, the patient's parents are taught the skills necessary to implement the therapy at home.

Patients work on changing one behavior at a time, and their progress is tracked by their parents in the form of a chart or other visual reminder that is displayed in a prominent place in the home. The child earns a gold star or a point on the chart for appropriate behavior. Some parents use a token, such as a button or poker chip. When a set number of symbols or tokens is earned, the child receives a special privilege or reward, such as a small toy or extra playtime. The goals are for children to learn which behaviors are acceptable and which are not and for them to eventually develop enough awareness to monitor their own behavior without the help of a chart or rewards.

Focusing attention on good behavior, rather than negative behavior, helps make this happen. Experts often advise parents to ignore inappropriate behavior when possible since many children behave badly to get attention. Teachers can also work with parents by using similar behavioral tactics with the child in school.

Because it is especially difficult to diagnose young children with ADHD accurately, the CDC and APA recommend using only behavioral therapy to treat children under the age of five. Children over the age of five respond well to a combination of drug and behavioral therapy. According to NIMH, medication alone, as well as medication and behavioral therapy together, result in the greatest improvement in ADHD symptoms in children. The multimodal approach is especially effective in modifying deliberately disobedient behavior, as well as improving interactions between children and all other people, including their parents, teachers, and peers.

The best ADHD treatment is one that is personalized for the patient and involves more than one approach, such as medication and behavioral therapy.

Unconventional Treatments

Counseling and behavioral training are, like medication, traditional treatments for ADHD. They are generally accepted by the medical community in the United States. Other ADHD treatments are less conventional and are often not accepted by traditional doctors. These are known as alternative treatments. Some forms of alternative treatment have been widely studied, while some have not. Conventional treatments such as medications undergo thorough testing and must be approved as safe for the public by the U.S. Food and Drug Administration (FDA), the government agency that regulates medicines. Alternative treatments, however, are not regulated by the U.S. government, so using them can be risky.

Despite these concerns, some people with ADHD turn to alternative treatments to help relieve their symptoms. Some patients combine alternative treatments with traditional treatment in a method known as complementary treatment, while others use alternative treatments in place of traditional treatments.

A number of traditional health care professionals believe that some alternative treatments can be beneficial in treating ADHD, especially when used in addition to traditional therapies. Clinical psychologist and ADHD expert Barbara Ingersoll explained, "Asking if you should use medication or complementary therapy to treat [ADHD] is like asking whether you should eat fruit or vegetables. You often need both."[28]

Herbal Supplements

Herbal therapy uses the stems, roots, leaves, bark, and seeds of plants known to have healing properties. A number of different herbs can be used to help treat ADHD symptoms in addition to other therapies. However, medical professionals should always be consulted before adding herbal supplements into a treatment plan, especially if they may negatively interact with other treatments. Two common herbal supplements include St. John's wort and ginkgo biloba. Although it is not known exactly how these herbs work, it is believed they contain substances that increase blood flow to the brain, raise levels of

neurotransmitters, enhance the activity of neurotransmitters, create a feeling of calm, or have a combination of these effects. They are taken in capsule or
liquid form, or as a tea. St. John's wort comes from
the flowers of the plant of the same name. Chemicals
in St. John's wort are thought to increase levels of the
neurotransmitter norepinephrine in the brain. Some
people with ADHD say St. John's wort makes them
feel more emotionally balanced. It calms them down,
relieves their anxiety, and lifts their mood. There is no
scientific evidence, however, to prove the herb actually
has this effect. A 2008 study at Bastyr University in
Seattle, Washington, found
that St. John's wort is no more
effective in treating the symptoms of children with ADHD
than a placebo. Still, many
people with the disorder say
St. John's wort helps them.

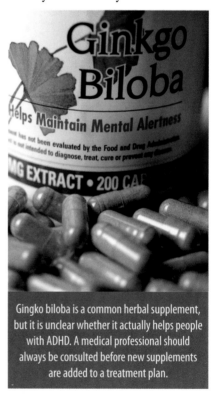

Ginkgo biloba is another
common herbal supple-
ment. Herbalists say it contains chemicals that increase
blood flow to the brain,
which appears to enhance a
patient's focus and memory.
Without more intense studies, it is unclear whether herbal treatments really improve
ADHD symptoms.

Gingko biloba is a common herbal supplement,
but it is unclear whether it actually helps people
with ADHD. A medical professional should
always be consulted before new supplements
are added to a treatment plan.

Omega-3 Fatty Acid

In addition to herbs, some people find that comple-
menting traditional ADHD treatments with nutritional supplements lessens their symptoms. Omega-
3 fatty acid, in particular, appears to have a positive
effect on ADHD symptoms.

Outdoor Activities

Scientists have found that being outdoors in a natural setting improves people's ability to concentrate and perform mental tasks. Using this knowledge, researchers at the University of Illinois at Urbana-Champaign conducted a study in 2007 to see whether spending time outdoors impacts ADHD symptoms.

University researchers had the parents of 406 children with ADHD track their children's weekend and after-school activities and note how these activities affected the children's behavior. When the children spent time indoors, their symptoms did not improve. When the children spent time in a natural setting, however, they were less restless and better able to focus their attention, complete tasks, and follow directions. In many cases, the children also slept better at night. An added benefit of this is that it also allows children to spend time outside being active with their friends, which has positive effects on weight, overall health, and social interaction.

It has been shown that spending time outdoors helps people's ability to concentrate and improves overall health.

Omega-3 fatty acid is a healthy fat that strengthens the immune system, helps brain cells develop and function, increases blood flow to the brain, and raises dopamine levels in the brain. The body cannot make omega-3 fatty acid but can obtain it from food or nutritional supplements. It is found in fatty cold-water fish, such as salmon, tuna, sardines, and anchovies; nuts and seeds; avocados; dark leafy vegetables; and certain oils. Nutritional supplements that contain omega-3 fatty acid include fish oil or flaxseed capsules.

A number of studies show that children with ADHD have lower-than-normal levels of omega-3 fatty acid in their bloodstream. One study conducted in 2008 at the University of Guelph in Ontario, Canada, measured omega-3 fatty acid levels in the blood of a group of adolescents diagnosed with

ADHD. The results were compared to the results of another group of adolescents of the same ages and weights that did not have the disorder. At the same time, the behavior of each adolescent was rated on the Conners Rating Scale. Not only did the ADHD group have significantly lower levels of omega-3 fatty acid in their blood than the control group, but there was also a correlation, or relationship, with blood levels and rating scores—the lower the blood levels, the poorer the scores on the rating scale.

In a 2007 University of South Australia study, 103 children with ADHD were given either an omega-3 fatty acid supplement or a placebo every day for 15 weeks. All the children were rated on the Conners Ratings Scale at the start of the study and again after 15 weeks. Researchers found that after 15 weeks, the scores of the omega-3 fatty acid group improved in impulsivity, inattention, hyperactivity, and social interaction. In comparison, there was no change in the control group's scores. Both groups were then given omega-3 fatty acid plus a multivitamin for an additional 15 weeks. Once again, all the children were rated on the Conners Rating Scale. This time, every child's scores had improved to such a degree that the researchers concluded that treating ADHD with omega-3 fatty acid is just as effective as Ritalin.

Although a few smaller studies in Europe have shown similar results, other studies have not. Experts caution that correlation does not equal causation;

Foods and supplements with omega-3 fatty acids in them, such as the ones shown here, have been shown to help a number of disorders.

in other words, it is not known if there is a direct cause-and-effect relationship between low levels of omega-3 fatty acid and ADHD symptoms. For this reason, health care professionals do not recommend substituting omega-3 fatty acid supplements for Ritalin. Researchers also say that it takes about six weeks before patients notice the effect of the omega-3 fatty acid supplement.

Benefits of a Healthy Diet

Eating certain foods and cutting back on others appears to help control ADHD symptoms, but diet alone cannot help the symptoms, nor is ADHD a result of a poor diet. White rice, cookies, cake, sugar, and simple carbohydrates found in processed snack foods and foods made with white flour break down quickly in the body. They create a quick burst of energy, which intensifies hyperactivity. They also cause a surge in blood sugar followed by a rapid drop. This lowers a person's ability to concentrate and worsens inattention. Complex carbohydrates found in whole grains, beans, and lentils, which break down slowly and do not cause blood sugar to spike, are a better choice.

Eating plenty of protein also prevents blood sugar surges. In addition, protein contains amino acids, which the body uses to make neurotransmitters. Many people with ADHD say that eating a protein-rich diet increases their ability to concentrate and decreases restlessness. Meats, fish, poultry, eggs, beans, seeds, and nuts are all good sources of protein.

While eating sugary foods is not what causes ADHD, a healthy overall diet involves eating fewer sugary foods such as those shown here.

Iron

Some individuals with ADHD also add more iron to their diet, either by eating more iron-rich foods or by taking iron supplements. Iron plays a key role in the production of neurotransmitters and helps regulate the flow of dopamine in the brain. Therefore, it is reasonable to theorize that an iron deficiency could lead to a chemical imbalance, which might cause

ADHD symptoms. A 2004 study by the University of North Carolina at Chapel Hill tested this theory. In this study, researchers measured iron blood levels in 53 children with ADHD and in 27 without. The iron levels of 87 percent of the children with ADHD were abnormally low, compared to 18 percent of the children without ADHD. The researchers also observed that the children with the lowest iron levels had the most severe ADHD symptoms. Based on these results, the researchers said that "low iron stores may explain as much as 30% of ADHD severity."[29]

Even if low iron levels do worsen ADHD symptoms, it is not known whether taking iron supplements improves these symptoms. Some individuals say iron supplements help, but there is no conclusive scientific evidence to prove this. What is known is that eating a diet rich in foods that contain iron is healthy. Such foods include meat, fish, poultry, eggs, whole grains, fortified cereals, legumes (beans and peas), vegetables, and certain fruits. Even if these foods do not reduce ADHD symptoms, they will have a positive impact on a person's mental and physical health.

The Danger of Supplements

Many people believe that because herbs and nutritional supplements are natural, they are safe and do not cause side effects. This is not true. Anything that is powerful enough to alter body functions can cause side effects and health risks, including herbs and nutritional supplements.

Herbs contain powerful natural chemicals. Many are as strong as drugs and, like drugs, they can cause a number of side effects. For example, St. John's wort can cause nausea, fatigue, anxiety, dizziness, headaches, and sun sensitivity. St. John's wort can also interact in the liver with certain medications, including antidepressants. This can cause toxic results when chemicals in the liver turn this combination into a poisonous and potentially fatal compound. In fact, it is illegal to sell St. John's wort in France due to herb-drug interactions.

Complicating matters, the lack of U.S. government regulations means herbs do not have set dosages. Therefore, herbal treatments may be weaker or stronger than patients anticipate. There have been cases in which herbal remedies have been found to be three times the strength written on the label. This can be dangerous. For instance, ginkgo biloba contains chemicals that thin the blood. High levels of the herb can inhibit the blood's ability to clot and cause dangerous bleeding. Another problem is that the ingredients in herbal treatments and their purity are not monitored. For example, while the leaves of ginkgo biloba are relatively safe to ingest, the seeds are poisonous, but there is no official agency checking to make sure that gingko biloba supplements do not contain any seeds.

Nutritional supplements, too, are not without risk. High doses of iron supplements, in particular, can be dangerous. Excess iron is not eliminated from the body. Instead, it circulates through the body and can weaken the body and cause disease. High levels of iron are linked to Parkinson's disease, a disease of the nervous system. For this reason, many health care experts advise patients to get their iron from food rather than from supplements.

No ADHD treatment is perfect, and alternative treatments are unproven. While some alternative treatments may provide additional relief from symptoms, it is always best to seek the advice of a medical professional before adding them into a treatment plan. Once a treatment plan is in place and the treatment starts working, the person may feel great relief. However, daily life with ADHD still presents some challenges.

CHAPTER FOUR

DAILY LIFE WITH ADHD

Diagnosing and treating ADHD can present problems for the person with the condition. It may take a long time before a diagnosis is received and an even longer time before a treatment plan is decided on. Once this happens, the person may encounter additional challenges, such as the stigma that comes with a diagnosis and treatment. However, with understanding and a helpful treatment plan, a person with ADHD can live a fulfilling life.

Adding Structure

Inattentiveness makes it hard for many people with ADHD to organize their thoughts, time, data, finances, and personal possessions. As a result, they tend to lose things, miss appointments, have trouble finishing tasks, and forget to do important things.

Disorganization is a real problem for many people with ADHD. The level of disorganization in ADHD sufferers is generally much greater than that of an average person. ADHD experts Hallowell and Ratey wrote, "We have trouble organizing things. We have trouble organizing time. We have trouble organizing thoughts. We have trouble organizing data. We put things in piles. We put time into limbo as we procrastinate … As inevitably as a match burning, we fall behind … We feel overwhelmed and inept. Incompetent. Lost. And so sad."[30]

Taking steps to add structure to their lives helps

individuals with ADHD feel more in control. Many of these steps are identical to those that people who do not have ADHD employ as organizational tools. The difference is that individuals with ADHD depend on these tools more than other people and use them to a much greater degree. Keeping to-do lists and notes and posting them in visible places, such as on the refrigerator, is one way people with ADHD remind themselves of what they have to do. "I have to put notes on the front door that I can't miss before I go out so I don't forget anything. When I cook, I write myself a note to make sure I remember I have something in the oven or I'd burn down the place,"[31] explained Ron, a man with ADHD.

Calendars, daily planners, or a cell phone are other tools individuals with ADHD can use to manage their time better. Besides recording appointments and deadlines, people with ADHD find it useful to record regular activities, such as an after-school sports practice. Otherwise, inattentiveness can lead them to forget such routine tasks. People with ADHD also use calendars, daily planners, and cell phones to help break up large assignments into several smaller tasks. This is known as "chunking." It is an effective tool for individuals with ADHD who are often unable to organize their time well enough to complete a large project. In addition, some individuals set timers or alarms on watches, clocks, and cell phones to help keep them on track and remind them of daily tasks.

Computers also help. Using a computer instead of writing things down allows individuals with ADHD to keep track of and file important information while minimizing loose papers, which are easily misplaced. According to Blake E. S. Taylor,

> *You can use a computer to help file and organize your papers and notes ... You can take notes on a laptop instead of taking notes by hand. Having the notes on your computer reduces your clutter factor*

significantly, and so you will become more organized. I have found that buying a laptop was the main way I solved my organization problem at school.[32]

Tools such as calendars and cell phones can help a person with ADHD stay organized.

Using a computer to handle personal finances is another step that brings structure into ADHD patients' lives. Computer programs that track finances and automatic bill paying are two measures that help. Since people with ADHD often forget to pay bills or simply lose them, such programs can be a lifesaver.

Designating specific areas for things such as schoolbooks, keys, and other items that can be easily misplaced is one more strategy that helps people with ADHD. Simple measures such as having a hook by the front door for keys, a basket for bills, or a special shelf for schoolbooks or work-related papers help people with ADHD get organized. "If you put something back where it belongs, it will be there when you next need it," Taylor wrote. "I'm always a little surprised when I put my books on their assigned shelves in the kitchen and then find them there the next morning when I'm stuffing things into my backpack."[33]

Physical Activity

Participating in physical activity is another way individuals with ADHD cope. Exercising focuses the mind

What Not to Say to Someone with ADHD

ADHD is a greatly misunderstood disorder, which may lead people to say things that are extremely hurtful to those who have been formally diagnosed and can even be hurtful to family members of these people. To reduce stigma and promote understanding of the disorder and how people who have it feel, a BuzzFeed contributor created a list of things that should never be said to someone with ADHD:

1. "Did you take your medicine today?"

2. "It's not that hard to just focus."

3. "ADHD isn't real."

4. "Calm down."

5. "Everyone is a little ADHD."

6. "My brother's friend's sibling's dog's pet sitter has ADHD so I totally understand."

7. "How could you forget that?"

8. "I think I'm ADHD too."

9. "Can I buy some of your meds?"

10. "You can't have ADHD, you're too smart."

11. "You need to act normal."[1]

1. Morgan Hendrix, "11 Things You Should Never Say to Someone with ADHD," BuzzFeed, April 1, 2014. www.buzzfeed.com/loudtallblonde/11-things-you-should-never-say-to-someone-with-adh-n6v4?utm_term=.arw-4JrRNN#.pgNjX9b33.

and allows individuals to release pent-up energy, which lessens feelings of restlessness. Moreover, exercising for at least 30 minutes causes the brain to release endorphins, which are natural chemicals that give the exerciser a feeling of well-being.

Like ADHD medications, exercise stimulates the production of dopamine and norepinephrine in the brain, which explains its positive effect on ADHD symptoms. The more vigorous the exercise is, the more powerful the results. Most individuals with ADHD find that regular physical activity improves their focus, mood, and problems with restlessness, which helps them to better meet the challenges they face.

Any form of physical activity helps relieve ADHD symptoms. Certain types of exercise, however—which involve movements that activate areas of the brain that control concentration, focus, evaluating consequences, timing, and sequencing—appear to strengthen connections between neurons in these areas of the brain. As a result, scientists theorize that frequent participation in these activities may have a positive long-term effect on ADHD symptoms. These activities include skateboarding, gymnastics, martial arts, skating, rock climbing, whitewater rafting, and dancing.

Researchers believe participation in physical activities can help relieve symptoms of restlessness that people with ADHD may feel.

Ways to Help Distraction

Exercise is just one tactic people with ADHD use to deal with restlessness. Feelings of restlessness make it difficult for people with ADHD to sit through meetings and classes or do their jobs properly. It can be hard for them to watch a movie or have dinner with friends. Seeking out activities that channel high energy and allow freedom of movement is a way for individuals to cope. This may involve centering social events around activities such as dancing or skating rather than sedentary ones such as going to the movies.

Combining a physical activity with a mental one also helps. For example, individuals may solve a

Multitasking, such as listening to an audiobook while cooking, can help people with ADHD improve their focus.

Background Noise

A 2007 Swedish study found that background noise, or white noise, helps people with ADHD concentrate. In this study, two groups of children, one group with ADHD and the other without, were given tasks that measured their concentration and memory level with and without white noise playing in the background. The researchers found that concentration and memory level improved in the children with ADHD when the white noise was playing. The non-ADHD children, on the other hand, performed better without the background noise. The researchers say white noise stimulates brain activity and increases dopamine levels. Since people with ADHD appear to have lower levels of dopamine and brain activity than those without the disorder, the effect of the white noise is to reduce ADHD symptoms and to help those with ADHD concentrate. Individuals without ADHD, on the other hand, already have high levels of brain activity and dopamine. Increasing these levels appears to overstimulate their brain and disturb their ability to concentrate.

problem while jogging, watch television while cleaning the house, or pace the room while planning a party. According to many individuals with ADHD, this strategy not only helps lessen restlessness but also helps turn off mental distractions, which improves their focus. This may be why many students with ADHD are most successful in hands-on, project-based classrooms where movement is part of learning.

Channeling energy into accomplishing something is another step individuals take. Cleaning the house, gardening, walking the dog, doing community service work, or playing an instrument, for example, all let individuals release energy in a positive manner. A 2006 Massachusetts Institute of Technology (MIT) study found that musical training helps improve brain functions. Blake E. S. Taylor plays the piano as a way to calm his mind and his body. "Classical music," he explained, "is very good ... Oftentimes, in the middle of my homework, I will go to the piano to play a Chopin étude or Mozart piano sonata piece. If I am nervous, I suddenly find I can relax and my mind seems better able to focus."[34]

Selecting a career that requires high energy levels is another important step. Doing so allows people with ADHD to turn what appears to be a problem into an advantage. Firefighting, law enforcement, acting, construction, teaching, nursing, landscaping, and farming are just a few examples of high-energy jobs.

For those circumstances when individuals with ADHD have to remain still, keeping an object handy that they can fidget with can help. One of Hallowell's patients said,

In certain careers, such as construction, high energy levels are an advantage, not a problem.

As a medical student, I spend a lot of time in lectures, studying, and talking to patients. So with all the listening I do, I need something to fidget with. My solution is Silly Putty. I have three eggs of Silly Putty. One egg lives in my book bag, so I can use it when I am in a lecture. One egg lives in the left pocket of my white coat, so I can reach in with my left hand and play with it while I am talking to a patient and still have my right hand free to take notes, and one egg lives at home on my desk where I can play with it when I am studying. Silly Putty is great. It's easy to un-stick from almost any surface, including fabrics; it's fun to play with, and it's cheap, so if I lose an egg, it's just a dollar to replace it. And because it's roughly the same color as my skin, it's unobtrusive.[35]

In 2017, fidget spinners were a huge craze. They were marketed as a way to help people focus and control disorders such as ADHD, but even people without the disorder enjoyed playing with them. The toys were sold in nearly every store as well as at events such as comic conventions, and they were available in many different

Fidget spinners became a short-lived popular item in 2017. While they were said to help with distraction and ADHD, they actually tended to be more of a problem than a solution.

designs. However, the claims that they improved focus were never scientifically proven, and the toys frequently created more of a distraction in the classroom, especially when multiple students were playing with them at the same time. According to Scott Kollins, a professor at Duke University and a clinical psychologist,

If their description says specifically that this can help for ADHD, they're basically making false claims because these have not been evaluated in proper research ... It's important for parents and teachers who work with kids who have ADHD to know that there are very well studied and documented treatments that work, and that they're out there, so there's not really quick and easy fixes like buying a toy ... It's important that people don't get into trying these fads when we do have treatments that can help these kids.[36]

Helping Sleeping Problems

Physical and mental restlessness and hyperfocusing can cause sleep problems for people with ADHD. When hyperfocusing, people with ADHD forget to sleep. Setting an alarm to go off at bedtime is one strategy that reminds people to go to bed.

Other measures involve making adjustments in the time of day stimulant medication is taken. Since these medications calm people with ADHD, taking a small dose an hour before bedtime allows many people with ADHD to get to sleep.

Drinking warm milk or eating a protein-rich meal

in the evening are other sleep strategies. Both are calming and prevent feelings of hunger, which often plague individuals with ADHD when the appetite-suppressing effect of stimulant medication wears off. Keeping the bedroom dark and cool also helps, as does listening to soothing music. Some people listen to recordings of nature sounds designed to give listeners a feeling of calm.

Support Professionals

Getting support from others is another way people with ADHD meet the challenges they face. Many turn to an ADHD coach, a specially trained professional whose job it is to motivate and help individuals with ADHD develop and implement strategies that help them cope with the disorder. Coaches help clients set up concrete goals and teach them specific strategies to achieve these goals. They collaborate with their clients, monitoring, guiding, and supporting them every step of the way. They support individuals when they fail, analyze why they failed, make suggestions on how to improve, keep individuals from giving up, help individuals identify and use their talents, and cheer on successes. ADHD coach Jodi Sleeper-Triplett, who coached a teenager named Rob for three years, said,

> I was originally hired ... to help with Rob's academics. It was the usual stuff for kids with ADHD. He wasn't into school. Wasn't taking his medication regularly ... Part of my role is to coach Rob with making choices, like when to go to a party, when to do homework, how to keep medication on track. Initially, we spent a half-hour on the phone each week ... A lot of our focus was trying to improve his organizational skills and time management ... What a coach does is put structure down in place for someone whose brain doesn't do it naturally.[37]

The Importance of Support

Many individuals with ADHD find that joining a support group helps, too. ADHD support groups consist of people with ADHD who share their experiences. Groups can be multi-age or consist of just adults or teens. Groups generally meet in public buildings, such as community centers, schools, or religious institutions, and are run by a mental health professional or someone with experience or training in working with people with ADHD. There are even internet groups for people who cannot attend meetings physically.

By sharing their common experiences, support group members learn coping strategies for problems that individuals without ADHD do not understand. Support groups also provide members with encouragement and a sense of belonging. Ari Tuckman, who ran an ADHD support group in Pennsylvania, said,

> *Don't underestimate the power of a support group ... Attendees [find] it helpful to tell stories, get advice, and share resources to help them at home, at work, and with friends. A good support group does something that nothing else does—it won't replace an understanding romantic partner or a knowledgeable therapist, but it will complement [add to] them nicely.*[38]

Meeting in a support group with other people who have ADHD can help those with the disorder talk to people who are going through the same things they are.

Children can find similar support in special summer camps for young people with ADHD. Being with children like themselves helps young people with ADHD feel less isolated and different. This builds their confidence and fosters positive self-esteem. Melissa Bailey sent her

11-year-old son, Jake, who was often excluded from social activities by his classmates, to an ADHD camp. Going to camp and finding peers like himself helped Jake feel accepted and more confident. According to Bailey, "For the first time he actually made friends. He participated in all sorts of outdoor activities, and came home feeling awesome about himself."[39]

In addition, specially trained staff members work with campers to develop skills to help them cope with their disorder. Through team-building activities, campers learn how to work with others and improve their social and organizational skills. Many ADHD camps also offer academic instruction for children with ADHD who have problems in school.

The Americans with Disabilities Act

People with diagnosed disabilities, such as ADHD, are automatically protected by the law in public places, such as restaurants, as well as in schools and places of employment. These legal protections ensure that people with disabilities, whether it is ADHD or another type of disability, are not discriminated against. The key to all of this is diagnosis—a person must be formally diagnosed and a medical professional must indicate that the symptoms the person is experiencing are severe enough to impair functioning.

The Americans with Disabilities Act (ADA) was enacted in 1990. The ADA

> is a civil rights law that prohibits discrimination against individuals with disabilities in all areas of public life, including jobs, schools, transportation, and all public and private places that are open to the general public. The purpose of the law is to make sure that people with disabilities have the same rights and opportunities as everyone else.[40]

The ADA is divided into five sections based on

different sections of public life—employment, public services (state and local government), public accommodations, telecommunications, and miscellaneous provisions. Some of the ways each section protects people with disabilities include:

- **Employment:** This ensures people with disabilities have the same employment opportunities and benefits as people without disabilities. In addition, employers are required to provide reasonable accommodations to qualified employees or applicants. This is defined as "a change to the job that accommodates employees with disabilities so they can do the job without causing the employer 'undue hardship' (too much difficulty or expense)."[41]

- **Public Services:** This part of the law prohibits discrimination by governments. Their programs, activities, and services must be able to accommodate individuals with disabilities. In addition, reasonable accommodations must be made to policies and procedures to avoid discrimination.

- **Public Accommodations:** This part of the law prevents private places, such as hotels, stores, restaurants, medical offices, day care centers, private schools, sports stadiums, movie theaters, and more from discriminating against individuals with disabilities. These businesses must make reasonable accommodations for people with disabilities and be able to effectively communicate with people who have vision, hearing, and speech disabilities.

- **Telecommunications:** This part of the ADA "requires internet and telephone companies to provide a nationwide system of interstate [between states] and intrastate [throughout one state] telecommunications relay services that allows individuals with hearing or speech disabilities to communicate over the telephone."[42]

• **Miscellaneous Provisions:** This section is a list of provisions for the entire ADA and includes its relationship to other laws and the impact on insurance benefits and providers. It also prohibits retaliation, or actions taken as a form of revenge, against individuals with disabilities.

Section 504 and IDEA

While the ADA does include educational protections for individuals with disabilities, there are two laws that are more specifically targeted toward education. These are Section 504 of the Rehabilitation Act of 1973 and the Individuals with Disabilities Education Act (IDEA). Section 504 is a civil rights law that

> covers qualified students with disabilities who attend schools receiving Federal financial assistance. To be protected under Section 504, a student must be determined to: (1) have a physical or mental impairment that substantially limits one or more major life activities; or (2) have a record of such an impairment; or (3) be regarded as having such an impairment. Section 504 requires that school districts provide a free appropriate public education (FAPE) to qualified students in their jurisdictions who have a physical or mental impairment that substantially limits one or more major life activities.[43]

The law also states that

> free appropriate public education is provided to each qualified student with a disability who is in the school district's jurisdiction, regardless of the nature or severity of the disability. Under Section 504, FAPE consists of the provision of regular or special education and related aids and services designed to meet the student's individual educational needs as adequately as the needs of nondisabled students are met.[44]

IDEA builds off of this law. Like Section 504, IDEA requires the availability of FAPE to students with disabilities. IDEA also ensures special education services and other related services to these students. IDEA was reauthorized by Congress in 2004, and in 2015, Congress amended IDEA through Public Law 114-95, which is the Every Student Succeeds Act. This act ensures that children have significant opportunity to receive a high-quality, fair, and equitable education. According to the U.S. Department of Education, IDEA's purpose is:

- *To ensure that all children with disabilities have available to them a free appropriate public education that emphasizes special education and related services designed to meet their unique needs and prepare them for further education, employment, and independent living;*

- *To ensure that the rights of children with disabilities and parents of such children are protected;*

- *To assist States, localities, educational service agencies, and Federal agencies to provide for the education of all children with disabilities;*

- *To assist States in the implementation of a statewide, comprehensive, coordinated, multidisciplinary, interagency system of early intervention services for infants and toddlers with disabilities and their families;*

- *To ensure that educators and parents have the necessary tools to improve educational results for children with disabilities by supporting system improvement activities; coordinated research and personnel preparation; coordinated technical assistance, dissemination, and support; and technology development and media services;*

> • *To assess, and ensure the effectiveness of, efforts to educate children with disabilities.*[45]

Special Education Services

IDEA is especially important for students with disabilities because it is the law that regulates and defines special education. It is also the law that requires public schools to provide these special education services to qualifying students between the ages of 3 and 21 who meet certain criteria, such as having a documented disability that IDEA covers and needing "special education in order to access the general education curriculum."[46] First, IDEA covers 13 types of disabilities as well as disabilities under the category of "other health impairment." The specific disabilities include disorders such as autism, intellectual disability, and dyslexia, while ADHD is often covered under the "other health impairment" category. Second, "access" is a very important term in education; it involves making the curriculum accessible for qualified students through modifications and accommodations.

Schools are required to place students and provide special education services in what is called the "least restrictive environment." Typically, this means starting the qualified student in a general education classroom with certain modifications in place and then moving forward from there. If this type of placement is not working well for the student, they may be moved into a different placement. By law, students with learning disabilities should be educated with students without disabilities as much as possible. To do this, strategies are implemented and outlined in the student's Individualized Education Plan (IEP), which

> *is a written statement of the educational program designed to meet a child's individual needs ... The IEP is developed by a team of individuals that*

includes key school staff and the child's parents. The team meets, reviews the assessment information available about the child, and designs an educational program to address the child's educational needs.[47]

An IEP is a binding contract that must be followed by the school district—it is a violation of the law to not follow a student's IEP. However, if they do not follow the student's IEP, it does not mean anyone will go to jail; instead, the school district is often found to not be in compliance and may have to provide additional services to compensate for those the student missed out on.

Some strategies that may be included in a student's IEP are:

- *Assistive technology* such as providing a laptop to help a student with a writing disability take notes in class

- *Accommodations* such as seating the student near the teacher (and far from distractions) or allowing [them] to give oral reports instead of writing essays

- *Modifications* such as reducing the amount of homework a student is assigned

- *Paraprofessionals* who serve as teachers' aides helping students with various tasks such as taking notes and highlighting important information[48]

If a general education classroom with strategies such as the ones outlined above is not the best placement for a student, they may be moved to a different placement. Possible placements include a self-contained classroom, inclusion classroom, and out-of-district placement. A self-contained classroom is a classroom with a lower ratio of students per teacher. For example, some ratios that may be used are 12:1:1 and 8:1:1, which means there are either 12 students or 8 students, 1 special education teacher, and 1 paraprofessional in the room.

However, these are not the only ratios used—there may be slightly more or fewer students in the room and more paraprofessionals. The benefit of this classroom is that the teacher can provide more one-on-one teaching and can tailor lessons to each student's goals and objectives that are outlined in the IEP. Students may spend all day in these types of classrooms, or they may spend most of their day in these classrooms and part of their day in general education classrooms for classes such as art, physical education, and music.

Different types of supports and classroom placements are available for students with ADHD to help them receive a quality education that accommodates their specific needs.

An inclusion classroom is a popular option at many schools. This classroom is a mix of students who receive only a general education curriculum and students who are receiving special education services. The class is typically taught by a general education teacher as well as a special education teacher. Each teacher shares equal responsibility for teaching the class and developing lessons, and they frequently weave in additional supports that may not be implemented in other classes of the same subject. The curriculum may also be modified according to skill levels and learning styles.

An out-of-district placement is for students who need more specialized teaching services than the school can provide. The student may be placed in a public school in a different district or a school that specializes in teaching students with disabilities. The last option may be a day school only, or students may stay on the school campus to receive all-day supports; however, they will not be taking classes all day. Given the fact that these schools specialize in teaching students with disabilities, the curriculum may be modified even more to account for learning styles, skill levels, and the objectives outlined in the IEP.

Can a Student Participate in an IEP Meeting?

There are periodic meetings to discuss the IEP, and students are encouraged to take part in them. This contract has a direct impact on the student's life, and students should advocate for themselves, take part in their education, and be vocal about their needs. This is especially important when the student is in high school and needs to think about what comes after. These are called transition goals. With these goals and meetings about transitioning, the student will be deciding what comes after high school. Do they want to go to college? If so, where do they want to go, and what do they want to major in? Do they want to learn a specific skill for a career? Do they want to get a job right after high school, and what type of job do they want? These are extremely important questions for the student to think about as they are preparing transition goals, and the answer to these questions will help school professionals determine how best to help the student and what can be done in high school to prepare them for the next step in their life.

CHAPTER FIVE

RESEARCH INTO ADHD

Despite scientific advancements and research, much is still unknown about ADHD. However, the years since it was first mentioned in scientific literature have provided researchers with plenty of new technologies to study the disorder and develop theories about its causes.

Identifying Genes

In an effort to identify genes common to individuals with ADHD but not to those who do not have the condition, researchers in Europe, South America, Asia, and North America conducted a study known as the IMAGE Project. In this study, researchers analyzed deoxyribonucleic acid (DNA), the chemical code for genes, taken from 1,400 families who have at least two children between the ages of 7 and 18, one of whom has been diagnosed with ADHD. The DNA was extracted from blood samples taken from each family member. It was examined, and the different genes found in the samples were recorded. Then, the findings were compared. Since most family members share many common genes, the scientists focused their attention on whether the children with ADHD carry gene variants or mutations that members of their family who do not have ADHD do not carry and whether other children with ADHD also carry these genes. To provide the researchers with a large pool of information and make it easier to identify specific genes relating to ADHD, all the findings were compiled in a database. According to Philip Asherson of the Institute of Psychiatry, King's College London, "The idea of the project is to create a resource that can be used both now and in the future to find the genes that cause ADHD. This is an exciting opportunity since the resource will be available to some of the best scientists in the world who wish to find the genes involved."[49]

So far, researchers have established that people with ADHD are more likely than other people to have variants of four genes: the dopamine transporter gene DAT1, which is involved in dopamine transmission, and the dopamine receptor genes SNAP 25, DRD4, and DRD5, which are involved in dopamine production and release. No single gene variant has been found in every child with ADHD, and some of the family members without ADHD carry one or another of these genes. Therefore, scientists do not think that the presence of any of these genes alone causes ADHD. They theorize that the presence of any one of these genes makes individuals more susceptible to the disorder, with susceptibility increasing with the number of variant genes a person carries. According to Asherson, "It is now established that variants of several genes occur more frequently in children with ADHD than in other children. None of these genes are necessary or suffi-

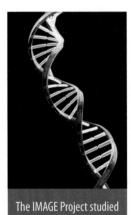

cient on their own to cause ADHD. Rather it is the cumulative effects of several genes."[50] As of 2017, the researchers had completed Study 5 of the project and joined the ADHD part of the Psychiatric Genetics Consortium. This group is gathering data from 47 studies, which includes the data of 500,000 genome markers for 80,000 individuals. The goal with this data is to analyze genetic disorder risk.

This is not to say that a specific gene that causes ADHD does not exist, but if it does, it has not been identified yet. With continued study, if there is such a gene, scientists may eventually find it.

The IMAGE Project studied the DNA of 1,400 families to compare gene variants and mutations with ADHD.

Genetic Screening Tests

In the meantime, researchers are using what they have learned to develop a genetic screening test that will establish whether young children carry any of the genes that make individuals susceptible to ADHD. Although such a test will not conclusively predict that a child will develop ADHD, it will show whether the child has a predisposition toward the disorder. This knowledge would allow the child's parents to take steps to minimize the severity of the disorder before symptoms arise. These steps include implementing behavioral therapy techniques, providing opportunity for physical exercise, and teaching the child structuring strategies. ADHD expert Susan Smalley of the University of California at Los Angeles said, "We believe that once we can identify children at risk for ADHD prior to the onset of symptoms we can help 'tailor' environments to minimize impairment and maximize the strengths of the ADHD child, adolescent, and adult."[51]

Researchers are looking into genetics to determine if children at risk for ADHD can be identified, which would help families and health professionals create a personalized treatment plan.

Treating ADHD

Currently, the methods for determining the right medication and dosage for individuals newly diagnosed with ADHD are imprecise. Genetic testing should help. A 2008 study at the University of Illinois used genetic tests to predict the effectiveness of ADHD medication. In this study, researchers focused on two dopamine transporter genes known as 9R and 10R. Individuals carry either a 9R or 10R gene, but not both. The researchers used genetic testing on 47 children ages 5 to 16 with ADHD to see which gene each child carried. Once this was determined, the researchers divided the children into two groups: those with the 9R gene and those with the 10R gene. Then they gave both groups varying doses of Ritalin and tracked how the drug affected the children.

The scientists found that the children with the 10R gene responded well to Ritalin. In contrast, the drug did not significantly improve the symptoms of the children with the 9R gene. Scientists do not know why, but they think that something about the 9R gene prevents individuals from responding to Ritalin. To learn more, scientists are conducting a larger study that will focus on how children with the 9R gene respond to other ADHD medications.

Other scientists are looking at genetic tests that identify genes that determine how quickly or slowly chemicals in the liver known as enzymes break down ADHD medications. If individuals carry genes that produce enzymes that break down the medication slowly, they will have higher-than-expected levels of the drug in their bloodstream, which increases the possibility and severity of side effects. On the other hand, if individuals carry genes that produce enzymes that break down the medication rapidly, they will have lower-than-expected levels of the drug in their bloodstream. Therefore, the drug will not be effective. Knowing how fast patients break down ADHD medication will make it easier for physicians to determine the appropriate dosage for patients.

Using genetic testing to determine how an individual will react to medication or a particular dosage is not yet a common practice, but scientists hope it will be in the future. This will take away a lot of the guesswork in ADHD treatment. According to University of Illinois head researcher Mark Stein,

Pharmocogenetics [the study of how genes and drugs interact] has great promise in ADHD, since the effects of medication range from a dramatic positive effect in many individuals while a minority display side effects or do not respond. Since ADHD often runs in families, it seems likely that genetics may play a large role in predicting medication response. But we're not yet at the point that we can use these findings in clinical practice. The hope is that eventually we can identify someone who is likely to benefit from a specific dose or at risk of having a severe side effect who could be treated more successfully with a different treatment approach ... It would be tremendous if we could scientifically predict medication response or non-response prior to treatment.[52]

Types of Brain Waves

There are five kinds of brain waves. All are measured at different frequencies, or speeds. Delta waves have the lowest frequency and produce the least brain activity. They exist at a frequency between 0 and 4 hertz, or cycles, per minute. Individuals produce delta waves when they are asleep. At frequencies up to 8 hertz, theta waves are slightly faster and produce slightly more brain activity. They are produced when people are in a relaxed or meditative state.

Alpha waves are produced when people are in a relaxed but alert state, such as when they watch television or read a magazine. They exist at frequencies up to 12 hertz. Beta waves, at 12 to 30 hertz, are fast, active brain waves. They are emitted when individuals are in a focused and attentive state. The fastest brain waves, however, are gamma waves, which exist between 38 and 42 hertz. They have been associated with unconscious mental activity, such as when people feel love, as well as advanced mental processing. People with ADHD appear to have too much theta activity in their brains and not enough beta, which corresponds to a lower-than-normal level of brain activity.

Neurofeedback Therapy

Since treating ADHD based on the presence of specific genes is still in the future, some scientists are developing treatments that can help people with ADHD right now. These treatments are based on brain science. One of the most promising is neurofeedback.

Neurofeedback is a process that trains individuals to change their brain activity. Individuals with ADHD appear to have lower-than-normal brain activity. Brain activity is measured in brain waves. The brain produces different types of waves. Those involved in concentration and attention create the most brain activity. Researchers theorize that through neurofeedback therapy, people with ADHD can learn to consciously produce the brain-wave patterns associated with focus.

To do this, patients are given various mental tasks to perform while electrodes are attached to their head. The electrodes, which pick up electrical signals produced by brain-wave activity, are connected to an electroencephalograph (EEG), a machine that records the signals. The signals are then sent to a computer with special software that creates a color-coded pattern similar to a graph. A mental health professional analyzes the pattern and then presents the patient with a series of exercises that helps increase brain activity. These exercises are made up of various video games, which require users to focus their attention in order to win the game. For instance, one game features an airplane that will only fly when players produce the appropriate brain waves. Scientists theorize that with neurofeedback therapy, individuals will learn what it feels like to focus and will be able to consciously change their brain activity in real-life situations.

A number of studies have been conducted to investigate the effectiveness of neurofeedback on people with ADHD. A 2006 University of Montreal study looked at how neurofeedback affected attentiveness and brain activity. In this study, 20 children ages 8 to 12 with ADHD were divided into two groups. One group was given neurofeedback therapy for 13 weeks. The other group received no treatment. None of the children took medication for ADHD during the study. The attentiveness of each child was rated one week before the study began and one week after it ended, using input from parents and the results of computerized attention tests. Brain scans were also administered while the children were taking the computerized attention tests. The first scans and attention ratings showed low brain activity and poor attentiveness in both groups. The second showed increased brain activity and attentiveness in the neurofeedback group, but not in the control group. According to Duke University research scientist David Rabner,

> *This study supports important new evidence to support the use of neurofeedback as a treatment for ADHD ... Improvements for treated children ... provide a stronger basis for suggesting the neurofeedback treatment was helpful. Most compelling of all, however, is the finding that neurofeedback treatment was associated with changes in brain activation detected by MRI scans ... Proponents of neurofeedback treatment have long suggested that it produces enduring changes in brain functioning, and it is these changes that cause ADHD symptoms to diminish. Results from this study provide important initial evidence consistent with this hypothesis.*[53]

Despite these results, the effectiveness of neurofeedback on ADHD symptoms has not yet been proven conclusively. Larger studies with more children and long-term follow-up are needed before it is known for sure if neurofeedback is a successful treatment.

Exercises for the Brain

Researchers in Sweden are focusing on other ways of training the brain. They have developed a mental exercise program that helps individuals with ADHD improve their working memory. Working memory is the ability to retain several facts or thoughts long enough to use them to solve a problem or accomplish a specific goal. In a broader sense, working memory allows individuals to use past events as a reference for dealing with current events. This helps them plan physical movements, regulate emotions, and organize their thoughts and surroundings.

Scientists theorize that people with ADHD have a deficit of working memory. Lead researcher Torkel Klingberg of the Karolinska Institute in Stockholm said that such deficits in individuals with ADHD "can explain why they forget the internal plan of what they are supposed to do next, or forget what they should focus their attention on."[54]

Therefore, the scientists theorize, improving working memory makes individuals more attentive and better able to solve problems. To train working memory, individuals are given increasingly more challenging computer-based mental exercises designed to improve attention. The exercises look and sound like video games. Individuals follow different exercise programs based on an assessment of their working memory. The exercises include activities that involve remembering and repeating words, numbers, or a sequence of events. The more events, words, or numbers trainees recall, the greater the number of items the trainees are holding in their working memory. The training is intensive. It takes place five days a week for an hour a day over the course of at least five weeks.

A 2005 study at the Karolinska Institute tested the effectiveness of working memory training on 53 children with ADHD who were not taking medication. At the start of the study, the children's working memory was evaluated via their performance on a span board, a device that tests visual and spatial memory. Then, half the children were given working memory exercises based on their individual working memory ability and told to work on the exercises every day for 25 days. The remaining children served as controls. Both groups were retested on the span board after 25 days and again 3 months after the study ended. The working memory group's scores improved significantly after 25 days. The improvement remained when they were retested three months later. The control group showed no improvement.

Moreover, an MRI of each child's brain taken at the start and end of a similar Swedish study showed physical changes in the training group's prefrontal lobe. It is the region of the brain most involved in thought and attention. Once again, these changes were not noted in the control group.

As of 2018, working memory training is available from a company called Cogmed. Other companies are working on developing similar programs. David,

ADHD in Hollywood

Having ADHD does not prevent individuals from achieving their goals. There are people with ADHD in all walks of life. In an effort to help and inspire others with the disorder, many well-known people have publicly acknowledged that they have ADHD.

One of the most famous of these people is singer Justin Timberlake. He stated in an interview that he has ADHD as well as obsessive-compulsive disorder (OCD) but prefers not to talk about this part of his private life in interviews.

Other famous people with ADHD include actor Channing Tatum, soccer star Tim Howard, and Maroon 5's Adam Levine. Levine has been more vocal than other celebrities about his ADHD and wants it to be known that ADHD typically does not always go away as one ages. According to Levine,

> My struggles continued as an adult. I had trouble sometimes writing songs and recording in the studio. I couldn't always focus and complete everything I had to. I remember being in the studio once and having 30 ideas in my head, but I couldn't document any of them. So I went back to the doctor to discuss my symptoms, and I learned that I still had ADHD. It was affecting my career the way it had affected me in school.[1]

Levine's interview shows that whenever a person feels something is wrong or they are having troubles with the continuing effects of something, they should always seek out a medical professional so they can find relief.

Singer Adam Levine has been open about his ADHD, which has helped people learn about it.

1. Adam Levine, "Maroon 5's Adam Levine: 'ADHD Isn't a Bad Thing,'" *ADDitude*, summer 2013. www.additudemag.com/adam-levine-adhd-is-not-a-bad-thing-and-you-are-not-alone/.

a 20-year-old man with ADHD, said that working memory training helped him. Before he started the training, he was working at a concession stand for the summer. Because of his disorder, it was difficult for him to work the cash register and remember incoming orders. He frequently gave the wrong change and confused the orders. Once he started the training, his memory gradually improved. By the end of the summer, he was able to do his job without making as many mistakes. As a result, he became more self-confident. Moreover, a year later, David said he still continued to benefit from the training.

About 75 percent of individuals who receive working memory training show improvement, and 80 percent of these individuals maintain their working memory gains for at least one year, with the level of improvement varying.

The Cerebellum

Other scientists are looking at a different form of exercise. They are investigating the effects of physical exercises that involve balance on ADHD symptoms. Such exercises stimulate the cerebellum, which mainly controls movement and balance. However, part of the cerebellum connects to the prefrontal lobe. Scientists think that at these connection points, the cerebellum is involved with the prefrontal lobe in learning, planning, and judging time. If, they theorize, the cerebellum could be stimulated, brain activity in this area of the cerebellum could be increased. This might help people with ADHD learn, plan, and manage time better. A 2005 Harvard University study that compared the brain activity of children with and without ADHD found that the children with ADHD had less brain activity in their cerebellum while doing a working memory exercise than the children without the disorder.

To stimulate the cerebellum, researchers have come up with exercises that involve the use of a balance board.

While standing on the board, exercisers are asked to juggle, move their eyes from side to side, and stand on one leg, among other exercises. Exercisers are instructed to perform the exercises twice a day for 10 minutes at a time for at least 6 months. Such exercises, according to ADHD experts Edward M. Hallowell and John J. Ratey, "draw upon the ability to balance, co-ordinate alternating movements, and perform actions that cross the midline of the brain and back again."[55] These seem to develop coordination and train the parts of the brain to work together, improving reading, attention, and organization.

A number of small British studies have tested the effects of cerebellum stimulation exercises on learning. None of the studies focused specifically on people with ADHD, but rather looked at the effect of the exercises on people with various learning difficulties, including ADHD. A 2004 study, which was conducted in public schools in Bedfordshire, England, compared the academic performance, behavior, and attentiveness of 36 students with learning difficulties who practiced the exercises for a year to students without learning difficulties who did not practice the exercises. At the start of the study, 60 percent of the exercise group exhibited ADHD symptoms. Both groups were evaluated with various tests before the study began and after it ended. The exercise group showed greater improvement in all areas than the non-exercise group. Moreover, at the close of the study, no one in the exercise group exhibited ADHD symptoms. More studies are currently being conducted. If the results are promising, cerebellum stimulation exercises may become a popular ADHD treatment option in the future.

New Studies Regarding Diagnosis

In 2017, a study was published in the journal *Radiology* that examined the possibility of identifying ADHD through MRIs. Currently, ADHD is diagnosed through symptoms, but it is an imperfect science. People who think they may have the disorder have to experience at least six months of symptoms before a formal diagnosis can be made, and some people go through life without a diagnosis or with the wrong diagnosis. This can lead to a lot of frustration for those with ADHD, so the possibility of diagnosing the disorder with brain scans is an exciting opportunity.

The research involves using cerebral radiomics, which uses information from the MRI to look for disease characteristics. The focus of the study was to establish classifications to assist in ADHD diagnosis, and 83 children who had been recently diagnosed with ADHD but never treated were the subjects. Researchers used information from these children and compared the results to children without ADHD. While there were no differences in the volume of the brain or gray or white matter, there were differences in three specific regions of the brain. The overall results of the study seem promising—based on the images and radiomic signatures, there was 74 percent accuracy in distinguishing between patients with and without ADHD. In addition, they were able to distinguish between inattentive and combined subtypes of ADHD with 80 percent accuracy.

Given these results, the researchers' goal is to recruit more people who have been newly diagnosed with ADHD to further confirm their results and also to learn more about classifications based on images. In addition, the researchers want to try to apply this information to other neurological disorders.

Using new technology, studies such as these not only prove that ADHD is a real disorder, but they can also get even more help for those who have been clinically diagnosed. With this wealth of scientific information, the stigma surrounding the disorder can start to be removed, and hopefully better treatment methods can be prescribed.

NOTES

Introduction:
A Real Disorder

1. Denise Foley, "Growing Up with ADHD," *TIME*, accessed November 29, 2017. time.com/growing-up-with-adhd/.

2. Ty Pennington, interview by Glenn Beck, *Glenn Beck Program*, July 22, 2008. www.glennbeck. com/content/articles/article/196/12741/?ck=1.

3. Foley, "Growing Up with ADHD."

4. Foley, "Growing Up with ADHD."

5. Anonymous, "In Your Own Words," ADHD Awareness Month, accessed November 29, 2017. www.adhdawarenessmonth.org/ survey-quotes/.

6. Kristen Bahler, "The 5 Best Jobs for People with ADD and ADHD," *TIME*, September 11, 2017. time.com/money/4935349/best-jobs-at-tention-deficit-hyperactivity-disorder-add/.

7. Edward M. Hallowell and John J. Ratey, *Delivered from Distraction*. New York, NY: Ballantine, 2006, p. xxxiii.

Chapter One:
Understanding ADHD

8. Kristin Koch, "What Causes ADHD? 12 Myths and Facts," Health.com, June 30, 2015. www. health.com/health/gallery/0,,20441463,00.html#chemical-exposure-0.

9. "Attention-Deficit/Hyperactivity Disorder (ADHD): The Basics," National Institute of Mental Health, accessed December 3, 2017. www.nimh.nih.gov/health/publications/attention-deficit-hyperactivity-disorder-adhd-the-basics/index.shtml.

10. Rachael Rettner, "Children with ADHD Share DNA Irregularities, New Study Says," LiveScience, September 30, 2010. www.livescience.com/35001-attention-deficit-hyperactivity-disorder-adhd-genetics-100929.html.

11. Hallowell and Ratey, *Delivered from Distraction*, p. 23.

12. Erica Roth and Rena Goldman, "Understanding ADHD Inattentive Type," Healthline, September 13, 2017. www.healthline.com/health/adhd/inattentive-type.

13. Roth and Goldman, "Understanding ADHD Inattentive Type."

14. Eloise Porter, "ADHD and Hyperfocus," Healthline, January 27, 2016. www.healthline.com/health/adhd/adhd-symptoms-hyperfocus#1.

15. Blake E. S. Taylor, *ADHD and Me: What I Learned from Lighting Fires at the Dinner Table*. Oakland, CA: New Harbinger, 2007, p. 26.

16. Quoted in "A Lifetime of Distraction," PriMed Patient Education Center. www.patienteducationcenter.org/aspx/HealthELibrary/HealthETopic.aspx?cid=L1004a.

17. "Basics of LD," Teaching LD, 2017. teachingld.org/pages/basics.

Chapter Two:
Diagnosing ADHD

18. "Adult ADHD (Attention Deficit Hyperactive Disorder)," Anxiety and Depression Association of America, accessed December 9, 2017. adaa.org/understanding-anxiety/related-illnesses/other-related-conditions/adult-adhd.

19. Marianne Kuzujanakis, "The Misunderstood Face of Giftedness," *Huffington Post*, April 10, 2013. www.huffingtonpost.com/marianne-kuzujanakis/gifted-children_b_2948258.html.

20. Quoted in Maria Yagoda, "ADHD Is Different for Women," *The Atlantic*, April 3, 2013. www.theatlantic.com/health/archive/2013/04/adhd-is-different-for-women/381158/.

21. Yagoda, "ADHD Is Different for Women."

22. Meadow Schroeder, "Signs of ADHD Can Be Different in Girls," CNN, November 27, 2017. www.cnn.com/2017/11/27/health/girls-adhd-signs-partner/index.html.

23. Hallowell and Ratey, *Delivered from Distraction*, p. 81.

24. Yagoda, "ADHD Is Different for Women."

25. Thomas Insel, "Post by Former NIMH Director Thomas Insel: Are Children Overmedicated?," National Institute of Mental Health, June 6, 2014. www.nimh.nih.gov/about/directors/thomas-insel/blog/2014/are-children-over-medicated.shtml.

26. Ariana Eunjung Cha, "CDC Warns That Americans May Be Overmedicating Youngest Children with ADHD," *Washington Post*,

May 3, 2016. www.washingtonpost.com/news/
to-your-health/wp/2016/05/03/cdc-warns-
that-americans-may-be-overmedicating-
two-to-five-year-olds-with-adhd/?utm_ter-
m=.488ec6644921.

27. Insel, "Post by Former NIMH Director."

Chapter Three: Alternative Treatments

28. Quoted in *The ADDitude Guide to Alternative ADHD Treatment*. New York, NY: New Hope Media, 2008, p. 2.

29. Quoted in Erica Lesperance, "Diet & ADHD: Are There Links Between ADHD & Diet?," Diet Channel, October 4, 2006. www.the-dietchannel.com/Diet-and-ADHD.htm.

Chapter Four: Daily Life with ADHD

30. Hallowell and Ratey, *Delivered from Distraction*, p. 328.

31. Ron, interview by Barbara Sheen, August 14, 2000.

32. Taylor, *ADHD and Me*, p. 41.

33. Taylor, *ADHD and Me*, p. 42.

34. Taylor, *ADHD and Me*, p. 54.

35. Quoted in Hallowell and Ratey, *Delivered from Distraction*, p. 312.

36. Quoted in Wynne Davis, "Whirring, Purring Fidget Spinners Provide Entertainment, Not ADHD Help," NPR, May 14, 2017. www.npr.org/2017/05/14/527988954/whirring-purring-fidget-spinners-provide-entertainment-not-adhd-help.

37. Quoted in Maureen Connolly, "I Almost Didn't Make It Through High School," *ADDitude*, August/September 2004. www.additudemag.com/high-school-college-substance-abuse-coaching/.

38. Ari Tuckman, "ADDA Support Group Manual," Attention Deficit Disorder Association. www.add.org/help/pdfs/SprtGrpManual07-07.pdf.

39. Quoted in Phyllis Hanlon, "ADDitude's Complete Guide to ADHD Summer Camps," *ADDitude*, April/May 2005. www.additudemag.com/adhd/article/837.html.

40. "An Overview of the Americans with Disabilities Act," ADA National Network, 2017. adata.org/factsheet/ADA-overview.

41. "An Overview of the Americans with Disabilities Act," ADA National Network.

42. "An Overview of the Americans with Disabilities Act," ADA National Network.

43. "Protecting Students with Disabilities," U.S. Department of Education, accessed December 10, 2017. www2.ed.gov/about/offices/list/ocr/504faq.html.

44. "Protecting Students with Disabilities," U.S. Department of Education.

45. "About IDEA," IDEA, accessed December 10, 2017. sites.ed.gov/idea/about-idea/.

46. The Understood Team, "Understanding Special Education," Understood, accessed December 10, 2017. www.understood.org/en/school-learning/special-services/special-education-basics/understanding-special-education.

47. "The Short-and-Sweet IEP Overview," Center for Parent Information and Resources,

August 1, 2017. www.parentcenterhub.org/iep-overview/.

48. The Understood Team, "Understanding Special Education."

Chapter Five:
Research into ADHD

49. Philip Asherson, "The Genetic Investigation of ADHD and the IMAGE Project," BBC. www.bbc.co.uk/sn/tvradio/programmes/horizon/adhd_genes.shtml.

50. Asherson, "The Genetic Investigation."

51. Quoted in "UCLA to Conduct Genetic ADD Research," *ADDitude*. www.additudemag.com/adhd/article/583.html.

52. Quoted in "Study Finds Genes May Predict Response to ADHD Medication," University of Illinois Medical Center at Chicago, March 2005. uillinoismedcenter.org/content.cfm/adhd_genes.

53. David Rabner, "New Controlled Study Shows Neurofeedback Helps Children Pay Attention and Improves Their Brain Functions," Peak Achievement Training. www.peakachievement.com/Default.aspx?PageID=1966808&A=-SearchResult&SearchID=244114&ObjectID=1966808&ObjectType=1.

54. Quoted in Keath Low, "ADD and Working Memory: Pump It Up! Working Out Your Working Memory," About.com, September 15, 2008. add.about.com/od/researchstudies/a/workingmemory.htm?p=1.

55. Hallowell and Ratey, *Delivered from Distraction*, p. 229.

antidepressant: A medication used to treat depression and several other mental illnesses.

basal ganglia: The part of the cerebrum involved in motor control, emotions, and learning.

behavioral therapy: Techniques used to change behavior.

brain scan: An image of the brain that is produced with various imaging devices.

cerebellum: The part of the brain involved with movement.

cerebrum: The part of the brain involved with thought.

chemical imbalance: Abnormal levels of neurotransmitters in the brain.

chunking: Breaking up large tasks into several smaller ones.

frontal lobe: The part of the cerebrum most involved in thought, focus, attention, and impulse control.

gene: The part of a cell that provides inherited information.

herbal therapy: Treatment with plants that are believed to have medicinal properties.

hyperfocus: A state of attentiveness in which all outside stimuli are blocked out of the mind.

magnetic resonance imaging (MRI): An imaging device that uses radio waves to produce an image of the brain.

neurofeedback: A process through which individuals learn to control brain activity.

neuron: A brain cell.

neurotransmitter: A chemical that transports information to the different areas of the brain.

stimulant: A medication that causes the user to feel mentally and physically alert.

working memory: The ability to retain several facts or thoughts long enough to use them to solve a problem or accomplish a specific goal.

Anxiety and Depression Association of America (ADAA)
8701 Georgia Avenue, Suite 412
Silver Spring, MD 20910
(240) 485-1035
information@adaa.org
adaa.org
The ADAA provides information on disorders such as anxiety and depression, which can occur with ADHD. Its website has a therapist directory and information on support groups. Always ask a parent or guardian before participating in events or online forums.

Attention Deficit Disorder Association (ADDA)
(800) 939-1019
adda@add.org
www.add.org
ADDA has an up-to-date website with information on ADHD, including ways to deal with it in everyday life.

Centers for Disease Control and Prevention (CDC)
1600 Clifton Road
Atlanta, GA 30329
(800) 232-4636
www.cdc.gov/ncbddd/adhd/index.html
The CDC's website has plenty of information about ADHD, including treatment, data and statistics, research, and diagnosis and treatment recommendations.

**Children and Adults with Attention-Deficit/
Hyperactivity Disorder (CHADD)**
4601 Presidents Drive, Suite 300
Lanham, MD 20706
(301) 306-7070
www.chadd.org
CHADD offers a wealth of information and support for
individuals with ADHD and their families. Its website
also offers a detailed resource directory organized by
state with information about professionals who specialize
in helping people with ADHD.

National Institute of Mental Health (NIMH)
6001 Executive Boulevard, Room 6200, MSC 9663
Bethesda, MD 20892
(866) 615-6464
www.nimh.nih.gov/health/topics/attention-deficit-hy
peractivity-disorder-adhd/index.shtml
The NIMH website includes information on
ADHD, education, treatment, and current research
on the disorder.

Books

Brown, Thomas E. *Smart but Stuck: Emotions in Teens and Adults with ADHD*. Hoboken, NJ: Wiley, 2014.
This book talks about ADHD and focuses on how emotions have a part in ADHD and daily functioning.

Flynn, Margaret C., and Peter Flynn. *Having a Learning Disability*. Mankato, MN: Smart Apple Media, 2000.
This book describes learning disabilities and daily life with them.

Honos-Webb, Lara. *The ADHD Workbook for Teens*. Oakland, CA: Instant Help Books, 2010.
This helpful workbook includes exercises, strategies, and worksheets for teens so they can find some relief from the common symptoms of ADHD.

Mooney, Carla. *Teens and ADHD*. San Diego, CA: ReferencePoint Press, 2017.
Mooney's book examines ADHD, how it affects daily life, what causes it, treatments, and strategies for those who have been diagnosed with it.

Spodak, Ruth, and Kenneth Stefano. *Take Control of ADHD*. Waco, TX: Prufrock Press, 2011.
This book includes strategies to help teens with ADHD in school, advice from teens living with the disorder, and how technology can help those with ADHD.

Websites

ADDitude
www.additudemag.com
This website has personal stories and a wealth
of strategies to help people with ADHD.

APA: What Is ADHD?
www.psychiatry.org/patients-families/adhd/what-is-
adhd
This part of the American Psychiatric Association's
(APA) website includes information on what ADHD is,
symptoms, treatment, diagnosis, and more.

KidsHealth: ADHD
kidshealth.org/en/parents/adhd.html
This KidsHealth website includes information on
ADHD for parents, kids, and teens.

LD Online
www.ldonline.org
This website provides information on various learning
disabilities, including ADHD, and has resource sections
and directories to find schools and professionals that
specialize in learning disabilities.

Understood: Understanding ADHD
www.understood.org/en/learning-attention-issues/
child-learning-disabilities/add-adhd/understanding-adhd
The ADHD section of the Understood website on
learning and attention disorders provides a variety of
information, including what ADHD is, how common it
is, and how professionals can help.

INDEX

Nicole Horning has written a number of books for children. She holds a bachelor's degree in English and a master's degree in special education from D'Youville College in Buffalo, New York. After earning her degrees and teaching certifications, she worked in special education classrooms, working with students who have disabilities such as ADHD, autism, and more. She lives in western New York with her cats, and in her free time, she volunteers with the Special Olympics Western New York division, writes, and reads.